A Greek Prose Reading Course for Post-Beginners

Unit 1. Forensic Oratory Lysias: *On the Murder of Eratosthenes*

With Commentary and Vocabulary by MALCOLM CAMPBELL

Bristol Classical Press

First published in 1997 by
Bristol Classical Press
an imprint of
Gerald Duckworth & Co. Ltd
61 Frith Street
London W1D 3JL
e-mail: inquiries@duckworth-publishers.co.uk
Website: www.ducknet.co.uk

Reprinted 1999, 2002

A catalogue record for this book is available from the British Library

ISBN 1-85399-537-1

Typeset by Malcolm Campbell

UNIT 1. FORENSIC ORATORY

CONTENTS

PREFACE

My thanks to John Betts for giving this project a warm reception and for very helpful advice, and to his team at Bristol Classical Press, Jean Scott, Editor, and Graham Douglas in Production, for welcome assistance with typesetting; to my colleagues Professor Stephen Halliwell and Dr Niall Livingstone for taking the time to read the typescripts and for suggesting a number of improvements; to my wife Dorothy for her encouragement, patience and technical help; to my younger son Richard for devoting more than one long evening to explaining to me what I was unable to work out for myself through reading *Macs for Dummies*.

No two teachers of Greek are likely to agree for long on how textbooks of this nature should be formatted, let alone what sort of information, and how much information, they should contain. I have been guided here first and foremost by our own students at St Andrews: I am grateful to them for discussing their difficulties and needs with me, for filling in questionnaires, and for producing some useful feedback on the form and content of earlier drafts of the Lysias and Plato texts. I must thank too a class of Bristol undergraduates whom I have never met, for offering general comment on the Lysias notes circulated to them in 1996 through the kind offices of John Betts and Onno van Nijf.

St Andrews, February 1997 M.C.

GENERAL INTRODUCTION TO THE COURSE

Represented in this course are three of the giants among prose writers of the Classical period, the historian Thucydides, the philosopher Plato, the orator Demosthenes. The same ancient literary critic (Dionysius of Halicarnassus) who called Demosthenes' *Philippic* iii "the greatest of the public orations directed against Philip" also found much to admire in the speeches of Lysias (see M. Edwards and S. Usher, *Greek Orators* I [Warminster, 1985], 128-9). There is certainly much to interest the modern reader in *On the Murder of Eratosthenes.*

In annotating these texts I have tried to keep the needs of three classes of reader constantly in mind:

Students fresh from Beginners courses (whether at University or elsewhere) reading an extended (and undoctored) Greek text for the first time.

Post-A-level (or equivalent) students who wish to consolidate their reading skills.

Postgraduate students who have some Greek but require guidance in reading an historical, oratorical or philosophical text in the original.

Since each unit is self-contained, those with an interest in Socrates, for example, can take on *Crito* right away. But post-Beginners are advised to read the Lysias speech before anything else: it is an excellent starter-text, and for that reason extra help has been given with the verbal systems. For the benefit of those who do choose to take on the course in its entirety the other three components have been given different emphases: in the Plato special attention is paid to the use of particles and particle-combinations, in the Demosthenes (a prime model for the few who still do Greek prose composition) to a number of key differences between Greek and English idiom; the Thucydides approximates more closely to the kind of commentary students will encounter if they carry their Greek studies further, with more extensive coverage of the subject-matter and explicit references to secondary literature. One possible programme, extending over two or three semesters: Lysias, Plato, Demosthenes and/ or Thucydides interspersed with a play of Euripides or Sophocles and a book or two of Homer.

For all four units the layout is essentially the same, and recommendations on study-methods are given in the respective prefaces:

1 Greek text. Observations are made from time to time in the Notes on the constitution of the text, and those who wish to pursue these matters further may consult the following editions, in which a critical apparatus (*apparatus criticus*) is

printed at the bottom of the page, where the editor, communicating in Latin, records variant readings in ancient and mediaeval copies (identified in the "Sigla" prefacing the text itself) and points to places where modern scholars have felt dissatisfied with the transmitted text and considered it necessary to emend:

Lysias, Oxford text by K. Hude (1912), see also the edition by C. Carey (1989), pp.12-13

Plato, Oxford text by E.A. Duke and others (1995)

Demosthenes, Oxford text by S.H. Butcher (1903), Budé text by M. Croiset (1955)

Thucydides, Budé text by J. de Romilly (1967), Oxford text by H.S. Jones and J.E. Powell (2nd edn, 1942).

2 Preliminary remarks on word formation and syntax geared to the text in question. Common to all: a systematic analysis of Perfects/ Pluperfects (usually viewed with dread by post-Beginners, in my experience), and a review of the uses of Subjunctive and Optative.

3 A brief outline of the entire work/ extract.

4 A summary of the content of each block of text.

5 Dedicated vocabularies, broken down into the various parts of speech. The words within each category are arranged alphabetically according to type: in the case of verbs, for example, infinitives in -ειν -εσθαι, then contracted forms -ᾶν -ᾶσθαι/ -εῖν -εῖσθαι/ -οῦν -οῦσθαι, and finally -ναι -σθαι.

6 Notes dealing with language, style and subject-matter.

7 It is envisaged that the material on each of the texts provided here will be topped up by tutors with a course of lectures dealing with author, genre, general background, broad issues and particular problems of interpretation. Those going it alone will find something to suit most tastes in the secondary literature specified in the suggestions for further reading.

ΛΥΣΙΟΥ
ΥΠΕΡ ΤΟΥ ΕΡΑΤΟΣΘΕΝΟΥΣ ΦΟΝΟΥ
ΑΠΟΛΟΓΙΑ

1 Περὶ πολλοῦ ἂν ποιησαίμην, ὦ ἄνδρες, τὸ τοιούτους ὑμᾶς ἐμοὶ δικαστὰς περὶ τούτου τοῦ πράγματος γενέσθαι, οἷοίπερ ἂν ὑμῖν αὐτοῖς εἴητε τοιαῦτα πεπονθότες· εὖ γὰρ οἶδ' ὅτι, εἰ τὴν αὐτὴν γνώμην περὶ τῶν ἄλλων ἔχοιτε, ἥνπερ περὶ ὑμῶν αὐτῶν, οὐκ ἂν εἴη ὅστις οὐκ ἐπὶ τοῖς γεγενημένοις ἀγανακτοίη, ἀλλὰ πάντες ἂν περὶ τῶν τὰ τοιαῦτα ἐπιτηδευόντων τὰς ζημίας μικρὰς ἡγοῖσθε. **2** καὶ ταῦτα οὐκ ἂν εἴη μόνον παρ' ὑμῖν οὕτως ἐγνωσμένα, ἀλλ' ἐν ἁπάσῃ τῇ Ἑλλάδι· περὶ τούτου γὰρ μόνου τοῦ ἀδικήματος καὶ ἐν δημοκρατίᾳ καὶ ὀλιγαρχίᾳ ἡ αὐτὴ τιμωρία τοῖς ἀσθενεστάτοις πρὸς τοὺς τὰ μέγιστα δυναμένους ἀποδέδοται, ὥστε τὸν χείριστον τῶν αὐτῶν τυγχάνειν τῷ βελτίστῳ· οὕτως, ὦ ἄνδρες, ταύτην τὴν ὕβριν ἅπαντες ἄνθρωποι δεινοτάτην ἡγοῦνται. **3** περὶ μὲν οὖν τοῦ μεγέθους τῆς ζημίας ἅπαντας ὑμᾶς νομίζω τὴν αὐτὴν διάνοιαν ἔχειν, καὶ οὐδένα οὕτως ὀλιγώρως διακεῖσθαι, ὅστις οἴεται δεῖν συγγνώμης τυγχάνειν ἢ μικρᾶς ζημίας ἀξίους ἡγεῖται τοὺς τῶν τοιούτων ἔργων αἰτίους· **4** ἡγοῦμαι δέ, ὦ ἄνδρες, τοῦτό με δεῖν ἐπιδεῖξαι, ὡς ἐμοίχευεν Ἐρατοσθένης τὴν γυναῖκα τὴν ἐμὴν καὶ ἐκείνην τε διέφθειρε καὶ τοὺς παῖδας τοὺς ἐμοὺς ᾔσχυνε καὶ ἐμὲ αὐτὸν ὕβρισεν εἰς τὴν οἰκίαν τὴν ἐμὴν εἰσιών, καὶ οὔτε ἔχθρα ἐμοὶ καὶ ἐκείνῳ οὐδεμία ἦν πλὴν ταύτης, οὔτε χρημάτων ἕνεκα ἔπραξα ταῦτα, ἵνα πλούσιος ἐκ πένητος γένωμαι, οὔτε ἄλλου κέρδους οὐδενὸς πλὴν τῆς κατὰ τοὺς νόμους τιμωρίας. **5** ἐγὼ τοίνυν ἐξ ἀρχῆς ὑμῖν ἅπαντα ἐπιδείξω τὰ ἐμαυτοῦ πράγματα, οὐδὲν παραλείπων, ἀλλὰ λέγων τἀληθῆ· ταύτην γὰρ ἐμαυτῷ μόνην ἡγοῦμαι σωτηρίαν, ἐὰν ὑμῖν εἰπεῖν ἅπαντα δυνηθῶ τὰ πεπραγμένα.

6 Ἐγὼ γάρ, ὦ Ἀθηναῖοι, ἐπειδὴ ἔδοξέ μοι γῆμαι καὶ γυναῖκα ἠγαγόμην εἰς τὴν οἰκίαν, τὸν μὲν ἄλλον χρόνον οὕτω διεκείμην ὥστε μήτε λυπεῖν μήτε λίαν ἐπ' ἐκείνῃ εἶναι ὅ τι ἂν ἐθέλῃ ποιεῖν, ἐφύλαττόν τε ὡς οἷόν τε ἦν, καὶ προσεῖχον τὸν νοῦν ὥσπερ εἰκὸς ἦν· ἐπειδὴ δέ μοι παιδίον γίγνεται, ἐπίστευον ἤδη καὶ πάντα τὰ ἐμαυτοῦ ἐκείνῃ παρέδωκα, ἡγούμενος ταύτην οἰκειότητα μεγίστην εἶναι. **7** ἐν μὲν οὖν τῷ πρώτῳ χρόνῳ, ὦ Ἀθηναῖοι, πασῶν ἦν βελτίστη, καὶ γὰρ οἰκονόμος δεινὴ καὶ φειδωλὸς [ἀγαθὴ] καὶ ἀκριβῶς πάντα διοικοῦσα· ἐπειδὴ δέ μοι ἡ μήτηρ ἐτελεύτησε, ἣ πάντων τῶν κακῶν ἀποθανοῦσα αἰτία μοι γεγένηται — **8** ἐπ' ἐκφορὰν γὰρ αὐτῇ ἀκολουθήσασα ἡ ἐμὴ γυνὴ ὑπὸ τούτου τοῦ ἀνθρώπου ὀφθεῖσα, χρόνῳ διαφθείρεται· ἐπιτηρῶν γὰρ τὴν θεράπαιναν τὴν εἰς τὴν ἀγορὰν βαδίζουσαν καὶ λόγους προσφέρων ἀπώλεσεν αὐτήν. **9** πρῶτον μὲν οὖν, ὦ ἄνδρες (δεῖ γὰρ καὶ ταῦθ' ὑμῖν διηγήσασθαι), οἰκίδιον ἔστι μοι διπλοῦν, ἴσα ἔχον τὰ ἄνω τοῖς κάτω κατὰ τὴν γυναικωνῖτιν καὶ κατὰ τὴν ἀνδρωνῖτιν. ἐπειδὴ δὲ τὸ παιδίον ἐγένετο ἡμῖν, ἡ μήτηρ αὐτὸ ἐθήλαζεν· ἵνα δὲ μή, ὁπότε λοῦσθαι δέοι, κινδυνεύῃ κατὰ τῆς κλίμακος καταβαίνουσα, ἐγὼ μὲν ἄνω διῃτώμην, αἱ δὲ γυναῖκες κάτω. **10** καὶ οὕτως ἤδη συνειθισμένον ἦν, ὥστε πολλάκις ἡ γυνὴ ἀπῄει κάτω καθευδήσουσα ὡς τὸ παιδίον, ἵνα τὸν τιτθὸν αὐτῷ διδῷ καὶ μὴ βοᾷ. καὶ ταῦτα πολὺν χρόνον οὕτως ἐγίγνετο, καὶ ἐγὼ οὐδέποτε ὑπώπτευσα, ἀλλ' οὕτως ἠλιθίως διεκείμην, ὥστε ᾤμην τὴν ἑαυτοῦ γυναῖκα πασῶν σωφρονεστάτην εἶναι τῶν ἐν τῇ πόλει. **11** προϊόντος δὲ τοῦ χρόνου, ὦ ἄνδρες, ἧκον μὲν ἀπροσδοκήτως ἐξ ἀγροῦ, μετὰ δὲ τὸ δεῖπνον τὸ παιδίον ἐβόα καὶ ἐδυσκόλαινεν ὑπὸ τῆς θεραπαίνης ἐπίτηδες λυπούμενον, ἵνα ταῦτα ποιῇ· ὁ γὰρ ἄνθρωπος ἔνδον ἦν· ὕστερον γὰρ ἅπαντα ἐπυθόμην. **12** καὶ ἐγὼ τὴν γυναῖκα ἀπιέναι ἐκέλευον καὶ δοῦναι τῷ παιδίῳ τὸν τιτθόν, ἵνα παύσηται κλᾶον. ἡ δὲ τὸ μὲν πρῶτον οὐκ ἤθελεν, ὡς ἂν ἀσμένη με ἑορακυῖα ἥκοντα διὰ χρόνου· ἐπειδὴ δὲ ἐγὼ ὠργιζόμην καὶ ἐκέλευον αὐτὴν ἀπιέναι, "ἵνα σύ γε" ἔφη "πειρᾷς ἐνταῦθα τὴν παιδίσκην· καὶ πρότερον δὲ μεθύων εἷλκες αὐτήν." **13** κἀγὼ μὲν ἐγέλων, ἐκείνη δὲ ἀναστᾶσα καὶ ἀπιοῦσα προστίθησι τὴν θύραν, προσποιουμένη παίζειν, καὶ τὴν κλεῖν ἐφέλκεται. κἀγὼ τούτων οὐδὲν ἐνθυμούμενος οὐδ' ὑπονοῶν ἐκάθευδον ἄσμενος, ἥκων ἐξ ἀγροῦ. **14** ἐπειδὴ δὲ ἦν πρὸς ἡμέραν, ἧκεν ἐκείνη καὶ τὴν θύραν ἀνέῳξεν. ἐρομένου δέ μου τί αἱ θύραι νύκτωρ ψοφοῖεν, ἔφασκε τὸν λύχνον ἀποσβεσθῆναι τὸν παρὰ τῷ παιδίῳ, εἶτα ἐκ τῶν γειτόνων ἐνάψασθαι. ἐσιώπων ἐγὼ καὶ ταῦτα οὕτως ἔχειν ἡγούμην. ἔδοξε δέ μοι, ὦ ἄνδρες, τὸ πρόσωπον ἐψιμυθιῶσθαι, τοῦ ἀδελφοῦ τεθνεῶτος οὔπω τριάκονθ' ἡμέρας· ὅμως δ' οὐδ' οὕτως οὐδὲν εἰπὼν περὶ τοῦ πράγματος ἐξελθὼν ᾠχόμην ἔξω σιωπῇ. **15** μετὰ δὲ ταῦτα, ὦ ἄνδρες, χρόνου μεταξὺ διαγενομένου καὶ ἐμοῦ πολὺ ἀπολελειμμένου τῶν ἐμαυτοῦ κακῶν, προσέρχεταί μοί τις πρεσβῦτις ἄνθρωπος, ὑπὸ γυναικὸς ὑποπεμφθεῖσα ἣν ἐκεῖνος ἐμοίχευεν, ὡς ἐγὼ ὕστερον ἤκουον· αὕτη δὲ ὀργιζομένη καὶ ἀδικεῖσθαι νομίζουσα, ὅτι οὐκέτι ὁμοίως ἐφοίτα παρ' αὐτήν, ἐφύλαττεν ἕως ἐξηῦρεν ὅ τι εἴη τὸ αἴτιον. **16** προσελθοῦσα οὖν μοι ἐγγὺς ἡ ἄνθρωπος τῆς οἰκίας τῆς ἐμῆς ἐπιτηροῦσα, "Εὐφίλητε" ἔφη "μηδεμιᾷ πολυπραγμοσύνῃ προσεληλυθέναι με νόμιζε πρὸς σέ· ὁ γὰρ ἀνὴρ ὁ ὑβρίζων εἰς σὲ καὶ τὴν σὴν γυναῖκα ἐχθρὸς ὢν ἡμῖν τυγχάνει. ἐὰν οὖν λάβῃς τὴν θεράπαιναν τὴν εἰς ἀγορὰν βαδίζουσαν καὶ διακονοῦσαν ὑμῖν καὶ βασανίσῃς, ἅπαντα πεύσει. ἔστι δ'" ἔφη "Ἐρατοσθένης Ὀῆθεν ὁ ταῦτα πράττων, ὃς οὐ μόνον τὴν σὴν γυναῖκα διέφθαρκεν ἀλλὰ καὶ ἄλλας πολλάς· ταύτην γὰρ [τὴν] τέχνην ἔχει." **17** ταῦτα εἰποῦσα, ὦ ἄνδρες, ἐκείνη μὲν ἀπηλλάγη, ἐγὼ δ' εὐθέως ἐταραττόμην, καὶ πάντα μου εἰς τὴν γνώμην εἰσῄει, καὶ μεστὸς ἦ ὑποψίας, ἐνθυμούμενος μὲν ὡς ἀπεκλῄσθην ἐν τῷ δωματίῳ, ἀναμιμνῃσκόμενος δὲ ὅτι ἐν ἐκείνῃ τῇ νυκτὶ ἐψόφει ἡ μέταυλος θύρα καὶ ἡ αὔλειος, ὃ οὐδέποτε ἐγένετο, ἔδοξέ τέ μοι ἡ γυνὴ ἐψιμυθιῶσθαι. ταῦτά μου πάντα εἰς τὴν γνώμην εἰσῄει, καὶ μεστὸς ἦ ὑποψίας. **18** ἐλθὼν δὲ οἴκαδε ἐκέλευον ἀκολουθεῖν μοι τὴν θεράπαιναν εἰς τὴν ἀγοράν, ἀγαγὼν δ' αὐτὴν ὡς τῶν ἐπιτηδείων τινὰ ἔλεγον ὅτι ἐγὼ πάντα εἴην πεπυσμένος τὰ γιγνόμενα ἐν τῇ οἰκίᾳ· "σοὶ οὖν" ἔφην "ἔξεστι δυοῖν ὁπότερον βούλει ἑλέσθαι, ἢ μαστιγωθεῖσαν εἰς μύλωνα ἐμπεσεῖν καὶ μηδέποτε παύσασθαι κακοῖς τοιούτοις συνεχομένην, ἢ κατειποῦσαν ἅπαντα τἀληθῆ μηδὲν παθεῖν κακόν, ἀλλὰ συγγνώμης παρ' ἐμοῦ τυχεῖν τῶν ἡμαρτημένων. ψεύσῃ δὲ μηδέν, ἀλλὰ πάντα τἀληθῆ λέγε." **19** κἀκείνη τὸ μὲν πρῶτον ἔξαρνος ἦν, καὶ ποιεῖν ἐκέλευεν ὅ τι βούλομαι· οὐδὲν γὰρ εἰδέναι· ἐπειδὴ δὲ ἐγὼ ἐμνήσθην Ἐρατοσθένους πρὸς αὐτήν, καὶ εἶπον ὅτι οὗτος ὁ φοιτῶν εἴη πρὸς τὴν γυναῖκα, ἐξεπλάγη ἡγησαμένη με πάντα ἀκριβῶς ἐγνωκέναι. καὶ τότε ἤδη πρὸς τὰ γόνατά μου πεσοῦσα, καὶ πίστιν παρ' ἐμοῦ λαβοῦσα μηδὲν πείσεσθαι κακόν, **20** κατηγόρει πρῶτον μὲν ὡς μετὰ τὴν ἐκφορὰν αὐτῇ προσίοι, ἔπειτα ὡς αὐτὴ τελευτῶσα εἰσαγγείλειε καὶ ὡς ἐκείνη τῷ χρόνῳ πεισθείη, καὶ τὰς εἰσόδους οἷς τρόποις προσίοιτο, καὶ ὡς Θεσμοφορίοις ἐμοῦ ἐν ἀγρῷ ὄντος ᾤχετο εἰς τὸ ἱερὸν μετὰ τῆς μητρὸς τῆς ἐκείνου· καὶ τἆλλα τὰ γενόμενα πάντα ἀκριβῶς διηγήσατο. **21** ἐπειδὴ δὲ πάντα εἴρητο αὐτῇ, εἶπον ἐγώ, "ὅπως τοίνυν ταῦτα μηδεὶς ἀνθρώπων πεύσεται· εἰ δὲ μή, οὐδέν σοι κύριον ἔσται τῶν πρὸς ἔμ' ὡμολογημένων. ἀξιῶ δέ σε ἐπ' αὐτοφώρῳ ταῦτά μοι ἐπιδεῖξαι· ἐγὼ γὰρ οὐδὲν δέομαι λόγων, ἀλλὰ τὸ ἔργον φανερὸν γενέσθαι, εἴπερ οὕτως ἔχει." ὡμολόγει ταῦτα ποιήσειν. **22** καὶ μετὰ ταῦτα διεγένοντο ἡμέραι τέτταρες ἢ πέντε, ... ὡς ἐγὼ μεγάλοις ὑμῖν τεκμηρίοις ἐπιδείξω. πρῶτον δὲ διηγήσασθαι βούλομαι τὰ πραχθέντα τῇ τελευταίᾳ ἡμέρᾳ. Σώστρατος ἦν μοι ἐπιτήδειος καὶ φίλος. τούτῳ ἡλίου δεδυκότος ἰόντι ἐξ ἀγροῦ ἀπήντησα. εἰδὼς δ' ἐγὼ ὅτι τηνικαῦτα ἀφιγμένος οὐδὲν [ἂν] καταλήψοιτο οἴκοι τῶν ἐπιτηδείων, ἐκέλευον συνδειπνεῖν· καὶ ἐλθόντες οἴκαδε ὡς ἐμέ, ἀναβάντες εἰς τὸ ὑπερῷον ἐδειπνοῦμεν. **23** ἐπειδὴ δὲ καλῶς αὐτῷ εἶχεν, ἐκεῖνος μὲν ἀπιὼν ᾤχετο, ἐγὼ δ' ἐκάθευδον. ὁ δ' Ἐρατοσθένης, ὦ ἄνδρες, εἰσέρχεται, καὶ ἡ θεράπαινα ἐπεγείρασά με εὐθὺς φράζει ὅτι ἔνδον ἐστί. κἀγὼ εἰπὼν ἐκείνῃ ἐπιμελεῖσθαι τῆς θύρας, καταβὰς σιωπῇ ἐξέρχομαι, καὶ ἀφικνοῦμαι ὡς τὸν καὶ τόν, καὶ τοὺς μὲν <οὐκ> ἔνδον κατέλαβον, τοὺς δὲ οὐδ' ἐπιδημοῦντας ηὗρον. **24** παραλαβὼν δ' ὡς οἷόν τ' ἦν πλείστους ἐκ τῶν παρόντων ἐβάδιζον. καὶ δᾷδας λαβόντες ἐκ τοῦ ἐγγύτατα καπηλείου εἰσερχόμεθα, ἀνεῳγμένης τῆς θύρας καὶ ὑπὸ τῆς ἀνθρώπου παρεσκευασμένης. ὤσαντες δὲ τὴν θύραν τοῦ δωματίου οἱ μὲν πρῶτοι εἰσιόντες ἔτι εἴδομεν αὐτὸν κατακείμενον παρὰ τῇ γυναικί, οἱ δ' ὕστερον ἐν τῇ κλίνῃ γυμνὸν ἑστηκότα. **25** ἐγὼ δ', ὦ ἄνδρες, πατάξας καταβάλλω αὐτόν, καὶ τὼ χεῖρε περιαγαγὼν εἰς τοὔπισθεν καὶ δήσας ἠρώτων διὰ τί ὑβρίζει εἰς τὴν οἰκίαν τὴν ἐμὴν εἰσιών. κἀκεῖνος ἀδικεῖν μὲν ὡμολόγει, ἠντεβόλει δὲ καὶ ἱκέτευε μὴ ἀποκτεῖναι ἀλλ' ἀργύριον πράξασθαι. **26** ἐγὼ δ' εἶπον ὅτι "οὐκ ἐγώ σε ἀποκτενῶ, ἀλλ' ὁ τῆς πόλεως νόμος, ὃν σὺ παραβαίνων περὶ ἐλάττονος τῶν ἡδονῶν ἐποιήσω, καὶ μᾶλλον εἵλου τοιοῦτον ἁμάρτημα ἐξαμαρτάνειν εἰς τὴν γυναῖκα τὴν ἐμὴν καὶ εἰς τοὺς παῖδας τοὺς ἐμοὺς ἢ τοῖς νόμοις πείθεσθαι καὶ κόσμιος εἶναι.” **27** οὕτως, ὦ ἄνδρες, ἐκεῖνος τούτων ἔτυχεν ὧνπερ οἱ νόμοι κελεύουσι τοὺς τὰ τοιαῦτα πράττοντας, οὐκ εἰσαρπασθεὶς ἐκ τῆς ὁδοῦ, οὐδ' ἐπὶ τὴν ἑστίαν καταφυγών, ὥσπερ οὗτοι λέγουσι· πῶς γὰρ ἄν, ὅστις ἐν τῷ δωματίῳ πληγεὶς κατέπεσεν εὐθύς, περιέστρεψα δ' αὐτοῦ τὼ χεῖρε, ἔνδον δὲ ἦσαν ἄνθρωποι τοσοῦτοι, οὓς διαφυγεῖν οὐκ ἐδύνατο, οὔτε σίδηρον οὔτε ξύλον οὔτε ἄλλο οὐδὲν ἔχων, ᾧ τοὺς εἰσελθόντας ἂν ἠμύνατο; **28** ἀλλ', ὦ ἄνδρες, οἶμαι καὶ ὑμᾶς εἰδέναι ὅτι οἱ μὴ τὰ δίκαια πράττοντες οὐχ ὁμολογοῦσι τοὺς ἐχθροὺς λέγειν ἀληθῆ, ἀλλ' αὐτοὶ ψευδόμενοι καὶ τὰ τοιαῦτα μηχανώμενοι ὀργὰς τοῖς ἀκούουσι κατὰ τῶν τὰ δίκαια πραττόντων παρασκευάζουσι. πρῶτον μὲν οὖν ἀνάγνωθι τὸν νόμον.

ΝΟΜΟΣ

29 Οὐκ ἠμφεσβήτει, ὦ ἄνδρες, ἀλλ' ὡμολόγει ἀδικεῖν, καὶ ὅπως μὲν μὴ ἀποθάνῃ ἠντεβόλει καὶ ἱκέτευεν, ἀποτίνειν δ' ἕτοιμος ἦν χρήματα. ἐγὼ δὲ τῷ μὲν ἐκείνου τιμήματι οὐ συνεχώρουν, τὸν δὲ τῆς πόλεως νόμον ἠξίουν εἶναι κυριώτερον, καὶ ταύτην ἔλαβον τὴν δίκην, ἣν ὑμεῖς δικαιοτάτην εἶναι ἡγησάμενοι τοῖς τὰ τοιαῦτα ἐπιτηδεύουσιν ἐτάξατε. καί μοι ἀνάβητε τούτων μάρτυρες.

ΜΑΡΤΥΡΕΣ

30 Ἀνάγνωθι δέ μοι καὶ τοῦτον τὸν νόμον <τὸν> ἐκ τῆς στήλης τῆς ἐξ Ἀρείου πάγου.

ΝΟΜΟΣ

Ἀκούετε, ὦ ἄνδρες, ὅτι αὐτῷ τῷ δικαστηρίῳ τῷ ἐξ Ἀρείου πάγου, ᾧ καὶ πάτριόν ἐστι καὶ ἐφ' ἡμῶν ἀποδέδοται τοῦ φόνου τὰς δίκας δικάζειν, διαρρήδην εἴρηται τούτου μὴ καταγιγνώσκειν φόνον, ὃς ἂν ἐπὶ δάμαρτι τῇ ἑαυτοῦ μοιχὸν λαβὼν ταύτην τὴν τιμωρίαν ποιήσηται. **31** καὶ οὕτω σφόδρα ὁ νομοθέτης ἐπὶ ταῖς γαμεταῖς γυναιξὶ δίκαια ταῦτα ἡγήσατο εἶναι, ὥστε καὶ ἐπὶ ταῖς παλλακαῖς ταῖς ἐλάττονος ἀξίαις τὴν αὐτὴν δίκην ἐπέθηκε. καίτοι δῆλον ὅτι, εἴ τινα εἶχε ταύτης μείζω τιμωρίαν ἐπὶ ταῖς γαμεταῖς, ἐποίησεν ἄν· νῦν δὲ οὐχ οἷός τε ὢν ταύτης ἰσχυροτέραν ἐπ' ἐκείναις ἐξευρεῖν, τὴν αὐτὴν καὶ ἐπὶ ταῖς παλλακαῖς ἠξίωσε γίγνεσθαι. ἀνάγνωθι δέ μοι καὶ τοῦτον τὸν νόμον.

ΝΟΜΟΣ

32 Ἀκούετε, ὦ ἄνδρες, ὅτι κελεύει, ἐάν τις ἄνθρωπον ἐλεύθερον ἢ παῖδα αἰσχύνῃ βίᾳ, διπλῆν τὴν βλάβην ὀφείλειν· ἐὰν δὲ γυναῖκα, ἐφ' αἷσπερ ἀποκτείνειν ἔξεστιν, ἐν τοῖς αὐτοῖς ἐνέχεσθαι· οὕτως, ὦ ἄνδρες, τοὺς βιαζομένους ἐλάττονος ζημίας ἀξίους ἡγήσατο εἶναι ἢ τοὺς πείθοντας· τῶν μὲν γὰρ θάνατον κατέγνω, τοῖς δὲ διπλῆν ἐποίησε τὴν βλάβην, **33** ἡγούμενος τοὺς μὲν διαπραττομένους βίᾳ ὑπὸ τῶν βιασθέντων μισεῖσθαι, τοὺς δὲ πείσαντας οὕτως αὐτῶν τὰς ψυχὰς διαφθείρειν, ὥστ᾽ οἰκειοτέρας αὐτοῖς ποιεῖν τὰς ἀλλοτρίας γυναῖκας ἢ τοῖς ἀνδράσι, καὶ πᾶσαν ἐπ᾽ ἐκείνοις τὴν οἰκίαν γεγονέναι, καὶ τοὺς παῖδας ἀδήλους εἶναι ὁποτέρων τυγχάνουσιν ὄντες, τῶν ἀνδρῶν ἢ τῶν μοιχῶν. ἀνθ᾽ ὧν ὁ τὸν νόμον τιθεὶς θάνατον αὐτοῖς ἐποίησε τὴν ζημίαν. **34** ἐμοῦ τοίνυν, ὦ ἄνδρες, οἱ μὲν νόμοι οὐ μόνον ἀπεγνωκότες εἰσὶ μὴ ἀδικεῖν, ἀλλὰ καὶ κεκελευκότες ταύτην τὴν δίκην λαμβάνειν· ἐν ὑμῖν δ᾽ ἐστὶ πότερον χρὴ τούτους ἰσχυροὺς ἢ μηδενὸς ἀξίους εἶναι. **35** ἐγὼ μὲν γὰρ οἶμαι πάσας τὰς πόλεις διὰ τοῦτο τοὺς νόμους τίθεσθαι, ἵνα περὶ ὧν ἂν πραγμάτων ἀπορῶμεν, παρὰ τούτους ἐλθόντες σκεψώμεθα ὅ τι ἡμῖν ποιητέον ἐστίν. οὗτοι τοίνυν περὶ τῶν τοιούτων τοῖς ἀδικουμένοις τοιαύτην δίκην λαμβάνειν παρακελεύονται. **36** οἷς ὑμᾶς ἀξιῶ τὴν αὐτὴν γνώμην ἔχειν· εἰ δὲ μή, τοιαύτην ἄδειαν τοῖς μοιχοῖς ποιήσετε, ὥστε καὶ τοὺς κλέπτας ἐπαρεῖτε φάσκειν μοιχοὺς εἶναι, εὖ εἰδότας ὅτι, ἐὰν ταύτην τὴν αἰτίαν περὶ ἑαυτῶν λέγωσι καὶ ἐπὶ τούτῳ φάσκωσιν εἰς τὰς ἀλλοτρίας οἰκίας εἰσιέναι, οὐδεὶς αὐτῶν ἅψεται. πάντες γὰρ εἴσονται ὅτι τοὺς μὲν νόμους τῆς μοιχείας χαίρειν ἐᾶν δεῖ, τὴν δὲ ψῆφον τὴν ὑμετέραν δεδιέναι· αὕτη γάρ ἐστι πάντων τῶν ἐν τῇ πόλει κυριωτάτη.

37 Σκέψασθε δέ, ὦ ἄνδρες· κατηγοροῦσι γάρ μου ὡς ἐγὼ τὴν θεράπαιναν ἐν ἐκείνῃ τῇ ἡμέρᾳ μετελθεῖν ἐκέλευσα τὸν νεανίσκον. ἐγὼ δέ, ὦ ἄνδρες, δίκαιον μὲν ἂν ποιεῖν ἡγούμην ᾡτινιοῦν τρόπῳ τὸν τὴν γυναῖκα τὴν ἐμὴν διαφθείραντα λαμβάνων **38** (εἰ γὰρ λόγων εἰρημένων ἔργου δὲ μηδενὸς γεγενημένου μετελθεῖν ἐκέλευον ἐκεῖνον, ἠδίκουν ἄν· εἰ δὲ ἤδη πάντων διαπεπραγμένων καὶ πολλάκις εἰσεληλυθότος εἰς τὴν οἰκίαν τὴν ἐμὴν ᾡτινιοῦν τρόπῳ ἐλάμβανον αὐτόν, σωφρονεῖν <ἂν> ἐμαυτὸν ἡγούμην)· **39** σκέψασθε δὲ ὅτι καὶ ταῦτα ψεύδονται· ῥᾳδίως δὲ ἐκ τῶνδε γνώσεσθε. ἐμοὶ γάρ, ὦ ἄνδρες, ὅπερ καὶ πρότερον εἶπον, φίλος ὢν Σώστρατος καὶ οἰκείως διακείμενος ἀπαντήσας ἐξ ἀγροῦ περὶ ἡλίου δυσμὰς συνεδείπνει, καὶ ἐπειδὴ καλῶς εἶχεν αὐτῷ, ἀπιὼν ᾤχετο. **40** καίτοι πρῶτον μέν, ὦ ἄνδρες, ἐνθυμήθητε· [ὅτι] εἰ ἐν ἐκείνῃ τῇ νυκτὶ ἐγὼ ἐπεβούλευον Ἐρατοσθένει, πότερον ἦν μοι κρεῖττον αὐτῷ ἑτέρωθι δειπνεῖν ἢ τὸν συνδειπνήσοντά μοι εἰσαγαγεῖν; οὕτω γὰρ ἂν ἧττον ἐτόλμησεν ἐκεῖνος εἰσελθεῖν εἰς τὴν οἰκίαν. εἶτα δοκῶ ἂν ὑμῖν τὸν συνδειπνοῦντα ἀφεὶς μόνος καταλειφθῆναι καὶ ἔρημος γενέσθαι, ἢ κελεύειν ἐκεῖνον μεῖναι, ἵνα μετ᾽ ἐμοῦ τὸν μοιχὸν ἐτιμωρεῖτο; **41** ἔπειτα, ὦ ἄνδρες, οὐκ ἂν δοκῶ ὑμῖν τοῖς ἐπιτηδείοις μεθ᾽ ἡμέραν παραγγεῖλαι, καὶ κελεῦσαι αὐτοὺς συλλεγῆναι εἰς οἰκίαν τῶν φίλων τὴν ἐγγυτάτω, μᾶλλον ἢ ἐπειδὴ τάχιστα ᾐσθόμην τῆς νυκτὸς περιτρέχειν, οὐκ εἰδὼς ὅντινα οἴκοι καταλήψομαι καὶ ὄντινα ἕξω; καὶ ὡς Ἁρμόδιον μὲν καὶ τὸν δεῖνα ἦλθον οὐκ ἐπιδημοῦντας (οὐ γὰρ ᾔδη), ἑτέρους δὲ οὐκ ἔνδον ὄντας κατέλαβον, οὓς δ' οἷός τε ἦ λαβὼν ἐβάδιζον. **42** καίτοι γε εἰ προῄδη, οὐκ ἂν δοκῶ ὑμῖν καὶ θεράποντας παρασκευάσασθαι καὶ τοῖς φίλοις παραγγεῖλαι, ἵν' ὡς ἀσφαλέστατα μὲν αὐτὸς εἰσῇα (τί γὰρ ᾔδη εἴ τι κἀκεῖνος εἶχε σιδήριον;), ὡς μετὰ πλείστων δὲ μαρτύρων τὴν τιμωρίαν ἐποιούμην; νῦν δ' οὐδὲν εἰδὼς τῶν ἐσομένων ἐκείνῃ τῇ νυκτί, οὓς οἷός τ' ἦ παρέλαβον. καί μοι ἀνάβητε τούτων μάρτυρες.

ΜΑΡΤΥΡΕΣ

43 Τῶν μὲν μαρτύρων ἀκηκόατε, ὦ ἄνδρες· σκέψασθε δὲ παρ' ὑμῖν αὐτοῖς οὕτως περὶ τούτου τοῦ πράγματος, ζητοῦντες εἴ τις ἐμοὶ καὶ Ἐρατοσθένει ἔχθρα πώποτε γεγένηται πλὴν ταύτης. οὐδεμίαν γὰρ εὑρήσετε. **44** οὔτε γὰρ συκοφαντῶν γραφάς με ἐγράψατο, οὔτε ἐκβάλλειν ἐκ τῆς πόλεως ἐπεχείρησεν, οὔτε ἰδίας δίκας ἐδικάζετο, οὔτε συνῄδει κακὸν οὐδὲν ὃ ἐγὼ δεδιὼς μή τις πύθηται ἐπεθύμουν αὐτὸν ἀπολέσαι, οὔτε εἰ ταῦτα διαπραξαίμην, ἤλπιζόν ποθεν χρήματα λήψεσθαι· ἔνιοι γὰρ τοιούτων πραγμάτων ἕνεκα θάνατον ἀλλήλοις ἐπιβουλεύουσι. **45** τοσούτου τοίνυν δεῖ ἢ λοιδορία ἢ παροινία ἢ ἄλλη τις διαφορὰ ἡμῖν γεγονέναι, ὥστε οὐδὲ ἑορακὼς ἦ τὸν ἄνθρωπον πώποτε πλὴν ἐν ἐκείνῃ τῇ νυκτί. τί ἂν οὖν βουλόμενος ἐγὼ τοιοῦτον κίνδυνον ἐκινδύνευον, εἰ μὴ τὸ μέγιστον τῶν ἀδικημάτων ἦ ὑπ' αὐτοῦ ἠδικημένος; **46** ἔπειτα παρακαλέσας αὐτὸς μάρτυρας ἠσέβουν, ἐξόν μοι, εἴπερ ἀδίκως ἐπεθύμουν αὐτὸν ἀπολέσαι, μηδένα μοι τούτων συνειδέναι;

47 Ἐγὼ μὲν οὖν, ὦ ἄνδρες, οὐκ ἰδίαν ὑπὲρ ἐμαυτοῦ νομίζω ταύτην γενέσθαι τὴν τιμωρίαν, ἀλλ' ὑπὲρ τῆς πόλεως ἁπάσης· οἱ γὰρ τοιαῦτα πράττοντες, ὁρῶντες οἷα τὰ ἆθλα πρόκειται τῶν τοιούτων ἁμαρτημάτων, ἧττον εἰς τοὺς ἄλλους ἐξαμαρτήσονται, ἐὰν καὶ ὑμᾶς ὁρῶσι τὴν αὐτὴν γνώμην ἔχοντας. **48** εἰ δὲ μή, πολὺ κάλλιον τοὺς μὲν κειμένους νόμους ἐξαλεῖψαι, ἑτέρους δὲ θεῖναι, οἵτινες τοὺς μὲν φυλάττοντας τὰς ἑαυτῶν γυναῖκας ταῖς ζημίαις ζημιώσουσι, τοῖς δὲ βουλομένοις εἰς αὐτὰς ἁμαρτάνειν πολλὴν ἄδειαν ποιήσουσι. **49** πολὺ γὰρ οὕτω δικαιότερον ἢ ὑπὸ τῶν νόμων τοὺς πολίτας ἐνεδρεύεσθαι, οἳ κελεύουσι μέν, ἐάν τις μοιχὸν λάβῃ, ὅ τι ἂν οὖν βούληται χρῆσθαι, οἱ δ' ἀγῶνες δεινότεροι τοῖς ἀδικουμένοις καθεστήκασιν ἢ τοῖς παρὰ τοὺς νόμους τὰς ἀλλοτρίας καταισχύνουσι γυναῖκας. **50** ἐγὼ γὰρ νῦν καὶ περὶ τοῦ σώματος καὶ περὶ τῶν χρημάτων καὶ περὶ τῶν ἄλλων ἁπάντων κινδυνεύω, ὅτι τοῖς τῆς πόλεως νόμοις ἐπιθόμην.

MORPHOLOGY AND SYNTAX

The following few pages, to which constant reference is made in the running commentary, focus on certain aspects of word-formation and syntactical structures. If you have an imperfect grasp of any of the areas covered, you will find it beneficial to study the data presented in the relevant section or sections *before* you embark on the text itself.

A. THE PERFECT AND PLUPERFECT

A.1

In Beginners' courses, the perfect and pluperfect generally crop up at a late stage, when there is mounting pressure to reach the final lesson. The former at any rate can prove a real distraction among other more general difficulties commonly encountered when an extended Greek text is tackled seriously for the first time. In fact, the perfect systems do not lend themselves to total assimilation within a very short time-span: one needs to work one's way into them, and to do that one has got to read a fair bit of Greek. A few moments spent (preferably with a set of paradigms illustrating the basic types by your side) on reviewing the perfects and pluperfects that actually occur in this speech may prove useful.

A.2.a

The important perfect εἰδέναι "to know" (from the same root as εἶδον, the aorist of ὁρᾶν) is so eccentric that it is better considered separately. We find:

Indicative 1st person singular οἶδ(α)

Infinitive εἰδέναι (2x), συν-ειδέναι

Participle εἰδώς (3x), εἰδότας

— Past tense (~ pluperfect):

1st person singular ᾔδη (2x), προ-ῄδη, 3rd person singular συν-ῄδει

A.2.b

It is convenient to consider at this point the verb κεῖσθαι ("to have been put", "to lie (down)"), since it serves as the *perfect passive* of τιθέναι ("to put"):

Indicative 3rd singular πρό-κειται

Infinitive δια-κεῖσθαι

Participle δια-κείμενος, κατα-κείμενον, κειμένους

— Past tense:

1st singular δι-εκείμην (2x)

A.3.a

— Active with *reduplication:*

Infinitive γεγονέναι (active form, from γίγνεσθαι: ctr. under A.5.a) (2x), δεδιέναι[1] ~

Participle δεδιώς[1], δεδυκότος (δύ(ν)ειν), πεπονθότες (πάσχειν); periphrastically to give 3rd plural indicative κεκελευκότες (κελεύειν) <§34: supply εἰσί from preceding ἀπεγνωκότες εἰσί>

— Active with *modified reduplication:*

Participle τεθνεῶτος (τεθνάναι[2])

— Active with *'Attic' reduplication* [3]*:*

Indicative 2nd plural ἀκηκόατε (ἀκούειν)

Infinitive προσ-εληλυθέναι (προσ-ιέναι/ -έρχομαι) and

Participle εἰσ-εληλυθότος (εἰσ-ιέναι/ -έρχομαι)

A.3.b

— Active with *(modified) augmentation/ irregularities:*

Indicative 3rd singular δι-έφθαρκεν (δια-φθείρειν), 3rd plural καθ-εστήκασιν (καθ-ιστάναι)

Infinitive ἐγνωκέναι (γιγνώσκειν)

Participle ἀπεγνωκότες εἰσί (ἀπο-γιγνώσκειν) periphrastically (see A.3.a above); and: ἑστηκότα (ἱστάναι), ἑορακυῖα[4] (ὁρᾶν), εἰκός[5] (ἐοικέναι)

A.4

— Pure Middle, only:

Participle ἀφ-ιγμένος (ἀφ-ικνεῖσθαι); periphrastically with εἴην to give 1st singular optative: πεπυσμένος (πυνθάνεσθαι)

A.5.a

— Passive with *reduplication:*

Indicative 3rd singular γεγένηται (γίγνεσθαι) (2x), ἀπο-δέδοται (ἀπο-διδόναι) (2x)

Participle γεγενημένου & -οις, ἀπο-λελειμμένου (ἀπο-λείπειν), πεπραγμένα & δια-πεπραγμένων ((δια-)πράττειν)

A.5.b

— Passive with *(modified) augmentation/ irregularities:*

Indicative 3rd singular εἴρηται (λέγειν)

Infinitive ἐψιμυθιῶσθαι (ψιμυθιοῦν) (2x)

Participle ἡμαρτημένων (ἁμαρτάνειν), ὡμολογημένων (ὁμολογεῖν), and παρ-εσκευασμένης (παρα-σκευάζειν), ἀν-εῳγμένης[4] (ἀν-οιγνύναι), εἰρημένων (λέγειν); periphrastically with εἴη to form 3rd person optative: ἐγνωσμένα [with neuter plural subject] (γιγνώσκειν)

A.6

The past of the perfect, the pluperfect, in its pure form: 3rd singular passive εἴρητο (λέγειν); periphrastically with ἦ to form active 1st singular ἑορακώς[4], passive 1st singular ἠδικημένος (ἀδικεῖν), with ἦν to form passive 3rd singular συν-ειθισμένον[6] (συν-εθίζειν)

[1] "to fear"/ "being afraid": these are "second perfect" forms, found alongside the "first perfect" forms δεδοικέναι and δεδοικώς. [2] "to be dead": τεθνεώς -ῶσα -ός is another "second perfect" type, coexisting with τεθνηκώς -υῖα -ός. [3] Where a verb beginning with a vowel reduplicates the initial vowel *and* consonant and lengthens the vowel that follows reduplication. [4] Notice the twin augmentation in -εῳγμένης; ἑόρακα is alternatively spelled ἑώρακα (in either case ὁρᾶν's aspiration is retained). [5] Remember that this is a *neuter singular* participle; the 3rd singular indicative is the very common ἔοικε(ν),"it seems". [6] Cf. the related perfect εἰωθέναι, "to be accustomed".

B. THE SUBJUNCTIVE

B.1

This section reviews all the uses to which the subjunctive is put in the course of the speech.

B.2.a

Final or purpose clauses, type "He does/ did this in order to be noticed". Straightforward: 7x in all (§§4, 9, 10, 11, 12 twice, 35), all introduced by ἵνα, negative μή, in primary (leading verb to be supplied in §12 ... ἵνα ...πειρᾷς) or secondary sequence.

B.2.b

Object clause with verb expressing a prospective fear, "be afraid that *x* may/ might happen": with μή ("that") + subjunctive, 1x (§44).

B.2.c

Object clause with verb voicing a request, in secondary sequence: "he implored and he begged not to be ...", ὅπως μή + subjunctive 1x (§29).

B.3

ἐάν (i.e. εἰ + ἄν) clauses, used to express:

(a) A prospective condition, type "[*protasis:* ἐάν + subjunctive] If you do so [viz. at some point in the future], [*apodosis:* future indicative] you will be punished". Examples in §§5, 16, 36, 47. But the apodosis harbours a *present* indicative in §5.

(b) A general condition or supposition, type "If somebody [in cases in which a person] acts thus, the law stipulates [as a general principle] imposition of the death-penalty". Examples: §§32 (a second ἐάν here with the verb to be mentally supplied), 49.

B.4

Indefinite clauses in primary sequence (ctr. under C.3), type "Whoever does this is automatically put to death" (remember that English often dispenses with the suffix "-ever"); 4x, introduced by the following, plus ἄν:

(a) A part of the ordinary relative pronoun ὅς (§§30, 35);
(b) ὅ τι, neuter of ὅστις, "whoever", §§6 and (ὅ τι .. οὖν, neuter of ὁστισοῦν, see note) 49.

B.5

Once only, μη(δέν) with 2nd person aorist subjunctive to express a prohibition, "do not/ don't you ..." (§18).

C. THE OPTATIVE

C.1

ἄν + optative (negative οὐ) in a hypothetical statement ("potential" optative), type "It would (could should etc.) be": 4x, §§1 three times (viz. ποιησαίμην, εἴητε, ἀγανακτοίη), 2 (εἴη).

C.2.a

The aforementioned brand of optative + ἄν in the *apodosis,* εἰ + optative in the *protasis,* in a condition of the type "If I were to do this, you would be angry". So in §1, protasis εἰ ... ἔχοιτε, apodosis οὐκ ἂν εἴη then ἀλλὰ .. ἂν ... ἡγοῖσθε.

C.2.b

In §44 οὔτε εἰ ταῦτα διαπραξαίμην, ἤλπιζον ..., the sense of the aorist optative is "nor, if I were to have (in the event that I should have) carried this out, was I entertaining hopes ..."

C.3

An indefinite clause in secondary sequence, ὁπότε + optative (§9), "every time that ..."

C.4.a

Indirect statement, in secondary sequence, type "I said that I was doing this", i.e. *present* optative (§19); or type "I said that I would do this", i.e. *future* optative (§22 καταλήψοιτο); or type "I said that I had done this", *perfect* optative (§18 εἴην πεπυσμένος, see under A.4 above). — A mixed bag in §20: *present* optative προσίοι (that "he made an approach to her", representing the tentative imperfect), then *aorist* εἰσαγγείλειε ("she had carried messages"), then another *aorist* πεισθείη ("had been prevailed upon"), then once again *present* προσίοιτο ("she was in the habit of bringing about his entrances") [the sequence is closed up with the vivid *indicative*].

C.4.b

Indirect question, in secondary sequence, type "He asked what was happening", so 2x *present* optatives in §§14, 15.

NOTES

For an excellent short introduction to Lysias and other representatives of the genre see M. Edwards, *The Attic Orators* (Bristol 1994); his first chapter deals succinctly with early oratory, oratory and rhetoric in the fifth and fourth centuries, deliberative, forensic and epideictic oratory, and the canon of ten Attic orators. — A section "Suggestions for Further Reading" is appended to the present Notes.

Before looking at each portion of the text, study the Vocabulary provided for it. It lists a number of words which are well worth committing to memory; those of lesser importance are dealt with in the running commentary. *Not* included are the very commonest words: any still unfamiliar to you as you work through the text should be looked up (try Liddell and Scott's *Intermediate Greek Lexicon*), jotted down and memorised at the earliest opportunity.

If you are having trouble with verbs, have a look at Appendices A-B.

"MS" refers to the introductory notes on Morphology and Syntax.

***

Synopsis

§§1-5 Introduction. The need to punish adulterers with the utmost severity. The requirements of the present case.

§§6-28 Narrative. The speaker, whose wife had been having an affair, was initially fooled into believing that all was well with his marriage. When he did get wind of the liaison, he resolved to catch the offender red-handed, and ended up killing him in the marital bedroom.

§§29-36 Arguments about the legality of his action.

§§37-42 Refutation of the charge that this was a case of entrapment.

§§43-50 Recapitulation capped not by a direct appeal for a favourable verdict but by a reaffirmation of the need to uphold the city's laws.

The case

The speech was delivered by one Euphiletus, an Athenian charged by the relatives of the young Eratosthenes with premeditated homicide (which carried the penalty of execution and confiscation of property: cf. §50); premeditated because, it was alleged, Eratosthenes did not just happen to be in Euphiletus' house on one of his frequent visits (as claimed by Euphiletus) to conduct an affair with the latter's wife, but rather was lured to the house, hauled into it and killed by the sacred hearth at which he had taken refuge (see §§27, 37; the speech for the prosecution is not extant).

Under homicide law (cf. §30) a man who caught a seducer in the act of having sex with his wife and killed him on the spot could not be convicted of murder. It may be inferred from §28 that the law specifying procedure in cases of adultery (which must be the law in question here) stipulated that homicide was lawful where the offender (a) was caught in the act and (b) admitted to the charge. Lawful, but not obligatory: alternative remedies were open to the aggrieved party (cf. on §25), and these do not figure at all prominently in the present speech. The suspicion that in Lysias' day summary execution was not generally resorted to, or that it was not generally regarded as the most reasonable or humane among the various means of redress, is strengthened by Euphiletus' insistence that he acted as an enforcer of civic justice, indeed that he was "commanded" by "the laws of the polis", the deterrent effect of which no responsible citizen would wish to undermine, to take drastic action. In other words, in this case, the jury is given to understand, an act of private vengeance administered by the victim must be regarded as an act of public punishment administered by a court of law: Euphiletus turns bedroom into courtroom at §§25ff.

On a more general level, at the start of the speech the point is made, obliquely, that *no* penalty is too severe for adultery (see the note on τὰς ζημίας in §1); and at the end (§49) "the laws" are said to stipulate that anyone who "caught" an adulterer (no "in the act" here) could deal with him "in *any* way he liked", this reinforcing a statement that the aggrieved party would be justified in resorting to "*any* means whatsoever" to catch such an offender (§37). Whether any member of the jury bore these general considerations in mind, and was moved to share Euphiletus' professed indignation at the outrageous and socially disruptive behaviour of a persistent (§16) offender, we shall never know; it is certainly hard to believe that all, or even a majority, could swallow (to take one notable example) the assertion that the accused, already determined to catch Eratosthenes red-handed, found it necessary to scurry about in the hours of darkness in a frantic attempt to round up witnesses.

§§1-5

Prooemium This falls into two parts. The speaker will have paused after §2, as with περὶ μὲν οὖν ..., "Well then, concerning ...", he closes up the topic of punishment and prepares (μέν) to consider the details of the offence. It is taken for granted at the outset that Eratosthenes has committed a shocking crime, with Euphiletus cast in the role of the victim who eventually triumphs over adversity. §§1-3 are concerned first and foremost with the need to deal with (§3: a "pardon" is out of the question), and to deal *severely* with, adulterers: this must be the universal feeling (πάντες §1 ~ ἅπαντας §3) not only among the Athenian jury-members but throughout the whole of Greece (ἁπάσῃ §2) and indeed among the entire human race (ἅπαντες ibid.).

The jury is expected to feel indignation at what has taken place (§1). We can detect the speaker's own sense of outrage in his insistent tone (§4): emphatic possessive adjectives (τὴν ἐμήν, τοὺς ἐμούς, τὴν ἐμήν, all postpositive with repeated definite article), emphatic third person pronoun (ἐκείνην), emphatic reflexive (ἐμὲ αὐτόν, "me personally"). To a string of offences (καὶ ... καὶ ... καὶ ...) is appended an emphatic denial of any sinister motive on the part of the accused (καὶ οὔτε ... οὔτε ... οὔτε ...). This long sentence is capped with a declaration that the punishment was in accord with "the laws". Finally (§5), the jury is reminded that the wronged Euphiletus' own life is now in danger (... σωτηρίαν), a point recalled at the close of the speech and related to observance of "the laws of the polis".

Vocabulary

Nouns

διάνοια, ἡ	notion, way of thinking
ἔχθρα, ἡ	hostility, personal animosity
ζημία, ἡ	penalty
σωτηρία, ἡ	(means of, chance of) salvation
τιμωρία, ἡ	redress, punishment (exacted in revenge or retaliation)
γνώμη, ἡ	opinion, view
~ συγγνώμη, ἡ	pardon
δικαστής, ὁ	juryman, juror
ὕβρις, ἡ	outrageous act, physical or verbal or both
[~ ὑβρίζειν	(with accus. person) commit such an act against]
κέρδος, τό	profit, gain
μέγεθος, τό	magnitude, severity
ἀδίκημα -ατος, τό	criminal act, offence

Adjectives

αἴτιος	(with gen.) responsible for
ἄξιος	(with gen.) deserving, worthy of
ἀσθενής	weak
πένης -ητος	poor

Verbs

αἰσχύνειν	disgrace
δια-φθείρειν	destroy; corrupt (a person)

ἐπι(-)τηδεύειν	engage in a practice, actively pursue a course of action
μοιχεύειν	See on §4 below
παρα-λείπειν	leave to one side, omit
ἀγανακτεῖν	be indignant, feel indignation (ἐπί + dat., on the basis of, at)
ἡγεῖσθαι	regard, believe
ἐπι-δεικνύναι	demonstrate, set out
Prepositions	
ἕνεκα	(+ gen., usually postpositive) for the sake of, because of
πλήν	(+ gen.) with the exception of
Particle	
τοίνυν	(postpositive) well then, therefore

Aids to comprehension

§1

περὶ πολλοῦ ἂν ποιησαίμην: A common idiomatic expression (cf. also in §26), "estimate at a high price", "value highly": "I would greatly appreciate".

ποιησαίμην: Seven optatives are crowded into §§1-2: see on these *MS* C.1-2.a.

ὦ ἄνδρες: 51 jury-members in a court called the Delphinium, set up to judge cases in which a defendant admitted homicide but claimed that his act was justified under the law (carried out ἐννόμως Demosthenes 23.74).

τὸ ... γενέσθαι: The accusative ὑμᾶς is *subject* of this articular infinitive (more positive than a conditional clause "if you were to ..."): "the fact that you ..." i.e. "your showing yourselves to be".

ἐμοί: "for me", "towards me/ in dealing with my case"; matched by the plural reflexive ὑμῖν αὐτοῖς, "you yourselves" (cf. ὑμῶν αὐτῶν shortly).

περὶ ... πράγματος: The speaker proceeds in a decidedly deliberate manner, availing himself on no less than six occasions in the course of §§1-3 of the dry περί in the sense "in connexion with", "in relation to".

οἷοί-: It is essential to grasp the function of οἷος: it is a *qualitative* relative (cf. in §47), here, as often, coming in the wake of the word for "such", "of such a nature": "the sort/ kind of person who ..."

-περ can lend sharpness to a relative (cf. below, and notes on §§27, 32-33, 39): "exactly", "precisely", "just".

πεπονθότες: Perfect participle, see *MS* A.3.a; πάσχειν, "experience", "have done to one": here "if you had been subjected to".

οἶδ(α): Cf. *MS* A.2.a.

τῶν ἄλλων: "the others", where we would say "(all) other people"; so commonly τἆλλα, "everything else".

(ἥν)περ ... i.e. hold the *very* same opinion ... as <you actually hold> ..., cf. on -περ above.

οὐκ ἂν εἴη ὅστις ...: "there could not be any person who could not ...", i.e. "there could not be a single one among you who could fail to ..."

τοῖς γεγενημένοις: Dative of τὰ γεγενημένα, cf. *MS* A.5.a.

ἀλλά: Strongly adversative: "but rather", "on the contrary".

τὰς ζημίας: "the penalties" must embrace all the possible ways (cf. the procedures noted on §25) of dealing with adultery, *including* the slaying of a man caught red-handed — a fact which Euphiletus chooses to skirt around both here, as he focuses on the outrageousness of Eratosthenes' conduct, and later in the prooemium, as he seeks to legitimise his actions (ἔπραξα ταῦτα he says in §4) with an appeal to "the laws".

μικράς: The opposite of μεγάλας (cf. μεγέθους in §3), "severe": (regard ... as) "lenient".

§2

εἴη ... οὕτως ἐγνωσμένα: "would be the considered/ accepted view": the perfect of γιγνώσκειν can signify "to have formed a judgement", "to have reached a (firm) verdict". — εἴη singular : neuter plural subject; for the perfect passive optative εἴη ἐγνωσμένα see *MS* A.5.b.

ἐν ... Ἑλλάδι: There is evidence that a hard line was taken with adulterers elsewhere (though not everywhere else) in the Greek world, but none of our sources for information of this kind is concerned with, for example, alternative means of redress or the question of possible softening of public attitudes with the passage of time.

ἁπάσῃ: The first of no less than five cases of this expanded form of πᾶς in the prooemium, all of them placed before the word(s) they govern.

τούτου .. μόνου: Exaggerating, "this ..., and this alone".

ἡ αὐτή: i.e. the same as that accorded to the strongest against (in dealing with) the weakest elements in society.

τοὺς τὰ μέγιστα δυναμένους: "those who have the greatest power/ influence" (τὰ μ., "adverbial" accusative, "in the highest degree").

ἀπο-δέδοται: Perfect passive of ἀπο-διδόναι (cf. *MS* A.5.a), "has been duly given", i.e. "is accorded as their due".

ὥστε ...: A fresh subject in this result clause, hence the accusative.

χείριστον serves as a superlative of κακός (here opp. βέλτιστος, a superlative of ἀγαθός); in social terms, "lowliest", "most humble".

τῶν αὐτῶν .. τῷ βελτίστῳ: "the same rights as <the rights accorded to> the most eminent/ highest"; "as": such is the force of the dative with ὁ αὐτός, cf. in §36.

τυγχάνειν *with genitive* (cf. in §3 below, and §27) means "get, obtain, be granted".

οὕτως ... δεινοτάτην: "so absolutely shocking".

ταύτην τὴν ὕβριν: "this <particular brand of> outrageous conduct".

§3

μέν is answered by δέ at the start of §4.

ὀλιγώρως διακεῖσθαι: The verb (cf. in general *MS* A.2.b), in conjunction with an adverb, means "be so disposed/ inclined, be of a certain disposition": "to be so permissive in his attitude" (adj. ὀλίγωρος: showing little or no concern, easy-going, casual to the point of negligence).

ὅστις οἴεται is used here in preference to a standard result clause (recently deployed) of the form ὥστε οἴεται, "as actually to believe that ..."

§4

τοῦτο: Emphatically placed: "that what I have to ... is this, namely that ..."

ἐμοίχευεν [act: μοιχεία; agent: μοιχός]: With accusative, "was having an illicit affair with", the affair in this case involving the seduction of another's man's wife.

διέφθειρε ... ᾔσχυνε: Imperfects, or aorists (see the flanking verbs)? The coordination suggests the latter: wife + children + self, the respective parties being subjected to moral corruption, social stigma and personal outrage, all as a direct result of μοιχεία.

παῖδας: A single child is mentioned in the subsequent narrative. Euphiletus, now up in arms, applies to his own particular case the general consideration that adulterers can cause problems for "the children" of a marriage (see §33).

εἰς ... εἰσιών: A point to which Euphiletus will return (§25, cf. §§38, 40). The intrusion into the house puts Eratosthenes on a par with a common thief, who could be killed legally if caught in the act (~ §36 ... εἰς τὰς ἀλλοτρίας οἰκίας εἰσιέναι).

εἰσ-ιών (~ εἶμι) serves as present participle of εἰσ-έρχομαι (cf. -ϊόντος in §11, -ιοῦσα in §13, ἰόντι in §22, -ιών in §23, -ιόντες in §24, -ιών in §25 and §39); so infinitive -ιέναι (§12 twice, §36), optative -ίοι (§20). Cf. Appendix A, under D.II.

ἵνα ... γένωμαι: Purpose clause, see *MS* B.2.a.

ἐκ: "from" to denote the transition from one state to another, "after being".

κέρδους: Supply ἕνεκα.

τῆς ... τιμωρίας: "the satisfaction in-line-with (sanctioned by) the law(s)". τιμωρία could well describe an act of *private* vengeance; the vengeance exacted by Euphiletus is a matter of civic justice: see in §47.

§5

ἐξ ἀρχῆς: "from beginning <to end>".

τἀληθῆ: Crasis (ἡ κρᾶσις, "coalescing"), for τὰ ἀληθῆ.

ταύτην rather than a neuter, anticipating the feminine predicate.

ἐὰν ... δυνηθῶ (aorist subjunctive of δύνασθαι): Prospective conditional clause, cf. *MS* B.3. This reinforces οὐδὲν ... τἀληθῆ: "if I can give you a *complete* picture of ...": a lengthy narrative is in the offing.

πεπραγμένα: Perfect participle passive, see *MS* A.5.a.

§§6-14

Narrative, part one. The story of how a harmonious and stable marriage is undermined by Eratosthenes, who gains access to Euphiletus' house and has an affair with his wife. She manages to fool her husband, so much so that even when something about her appearance does strike him as odd he offers no comment and goes about his business.

Vocabulary

Nouns

θεράπαινα, ἡ	servant-girl, maidservant
σιωπή, ἡ	silence; adv. -ῇ silently, without comment
ἀγρός, ὁ	the country
λύχνος, ὁ	lamp
δεῖπνον, τό	dinner
παιδίον, τό	(young) child
πρόσωπον, τό	face
γείτων -ονος, ὁ	neighbour

Adjectives

ἄσμενος	glad(ly)
σώφρων -ονος	virtuous, chaste

Verbs

βαδίζειν	go (usually on foot)
καθ-εύδειν	lie down to sleep, sleep
κατα-βαίνειν	go down, descend
κινδυνεύειν	incur danger
κλάειν	cry, weep
μεθύειν	be intoxicated
παίζειν	play/ fool about, joke
προσ-έχειν (τὸν νοῦν)	give (one) attention, devote attention (to one)

ὑπ-οπτεύειν	suspect, feel suspicion
φάσκειν	claim, assert
οἴχεσθαι	be gone, have gone
ὀργίζεσθαι	get angry
βοᾶν	shout, bawl
γελᾶν	laugh
σιωπᾶν	be silent, observe silence
τελευτᾶν	finish off; with τὸν βίον mentally supplied, die
δι-αιτᾶσθαι	lead one's life, live
ἀκολουθεῖν	(with dat.) follow, be in attendance on
δι-οικεῖν	manage, administer, control
λυπεῖν	harass, annoy, irritate
ψοφεῖν	make a noise (ψόφος)
δι-ηγεῖσθαι	describe, explain in detail
ἐν-θυμεῖσθαι	think about, reflect on (with gen.)
προσ-ποιεῖσθαι	pretend
ἀν-οιγνύναι	open
παρα-διδόναι	hand over, entrust
ἐρέσθαι	(an aorist, indicative ἠρόμην) ask, put a question
Adverbs	
ἀκριβῶς	with precision, strict care, meticulously
ἀπροσδοκήτως	unexpectedly
ἄνω	above, in an upper position, upstairs, opp. κάτω
εἶτα	next, then; then (as a consequence)
ἔνδον	inside, indoors, opp. ἔξω
ἐπίτηδες	on purpose, deliberately
λίαν	too much, excessively
νύκτωρ	during the night
Particle	
ὅμως	nevertheless, none the less

Aids to comprehension

§6

γάρ very often follows declarations of the type "I shall tell you (the truth)", and also exhortations such as "pay attention", "consider", cf. in §37 and §43; here an introductory "now" would fit the bill.

ἔδοξέ μοι: The aorist of this verb is regularly used of reaching a formal decision: "once I had made up my mind to ..."

γῆμαι: Aorist infinitive, "to get married".

ἠγαγόμην: The middle ἄγεσθαι is a common term for the introduction of a wife into one's household.

τὸν ... χρόνον: Accusative marking duration of time (cf. πολὺν χρόνον in §10, τριάκονθ' ἡμέρας in §14), "for the remaining period", up to the point specified by ἐπειδὴ ... below, i.e. "for the time being".

οὕτω διεκείμην ὥστε ...: Cf. on διακεῖσθαι in §3; "I was disposed not to ...", "my attitude was this, that I should ..."

μήτε ... εἶναι: There is a switch from the implicit personal subject of the infinitive λυπεῖν to an impersonal construction: "nor that it should be too much in her power", i.e. "nor to allow her too much freedom" to ...

ὅ τι ἂν ἐθέλῃ: On the use of the subjunctive see *MS* B.4; although the sentence as a whole is cast in secondary sequence, this clause is dependent on *present* infinitive ποιεῖν.

(ἐφύλαττόν) τε: Here a connective, "and".

ὡς οἷόν τε ἦν: "as it was possible", i.e. "as far as was practicable".

-εῖχον: Cf. on εἶλκες in §12.

εἰκός is a neuter perfect participle, *MS* A.3.b: "reasonable".

μοι ... underlines the point that the child was his own: his wife's illicit liaison lies in the future.

γίγνεται: The so-called "historic" present (cf. διαφθείρεται in §8, and further examples in §15, etc.), generally unacceptable in literary English: "was born".

ἐπίστευον ἤδη: "from this point on I began to ..."; then aorist παρέδωκα, marking the grand gesture of a single transfer of responsibilities.

πάντα τὰ ἐμαυτοῦ: "the management of all my own <domestic> affairs".

ἡγούμενος ... εἶναι: "considering that this was the strongest bond of intimacy there could be between us" (οἰκειότης: adj. οἰκεῖος "closely related, on intimate terms").

§7

καὶ γάρ: "since <she was> in point of fact".

οἰκονόμος ... φειδωλός: "a skilful [ctr. δεινοτάτην in §2] and thrifty [~ φείδεσθαι, "to spare", "be sparing"] household-manager". The bracketed ἀγαθὴ marks an interpolation in all manuscripts (an inept attempt, it would appear, to ensure that φειδωλός did not give the wrong impression: as a noun it can mean "miser").

μοι: Dative personal pronouns with possessive force ("my" etc.) are frequently encountered in conjunction with substantives denoting family-members.

ἡ ... ἀποθανοῦσα ... γεγένηται: "who having died has turned out to be", "who by her death/ whose death has proved to be". After γεγένηται the speaker breaks off in mid-sentence, hurrying on to the "hot" topic of events at the funeral: note the peevish ἡ ἐμὴ γυνὴ ... τούτου τοῦ ἀνθρώπου in the immediate sequel.

γεγένηται: For this perfect passive see *MS* A.5.a.

§8

ἐπ' ... ὀφθεῖσα: "because it was when she followed her for (at) her funeral procession [ἐκ-φορά, "the act of carrying out" the body] that she was spotted [ὀφθεῖσα from ὁρᾶν] ... and ..." The secluded middle-class Athenian housewife can come out into the open for the funeral of a close relative, as she can for a religious festival confined to women (see in §20).

ἀνθρώπου: Derogatory, "fellow" (cf. in §11).

χρόνῳ: "in due course", "eventually".

ἐπι-τηρῶν: "by looking out for".

ἀγοράν: Where the shopping was done.

λόγους προσ-φέρων: "by conveying messages/ proposals to her [the wife] <through this servant>".

ἀπώλεσεν αὐτήν: "brought about her ruin"; αὐτήν is the *wife,* not the girl.

§9

πρῶτον μὲν οὖν: We often wait in vain for something to pick up the formula "now in the first place".

οἰκίδιον: A *diminutive* of οἰκία, suggesting "a modest house".

ἔστι μοι: "there is to me', i.e. "I am the owner of".

διπλοῦν: διπλοῦς (contracted from -πλόος) = "double": "on two floors".

ἴσα ... ἀνδρωνῖτιν: Literally "having the upper parts equal to the lower in relation to the women's quarters and in relation to the men's quarters", i.e. "the women's quarters on the upper level being equal in area to the men's quarters on the lower level": so it was a simple matter to change them round.

ἐθήλαζεν: θηλάζω = "breast-feed" (~ θηλή "nipple").

ἵνα .. μή introducing a purpose clause (more in §§10, 11, 12 twice), cf. *MS* B.2.a.

ὁπότε .. δέοι: Indefinite clause, optative (δέοι of δεῖ) in secondary sequence (*MS* C.3): "every time <the child> needed to be washed [λοῦσθαι for λούεσθαι]".

κλίμακος: "ladder", here "(open) staircase", inside what was normally the male quarters rather than outside in the courtyard.

§10

οὕτως .. συνειθισμένον ἦν: On the "periphrastic" pluperfect see *MS* A.6; συν-εθίζεσθαι, "to become customary": "it had become such a regular practice, such a familiar routine".

ἀπ-ῄει (ἄπειμι ~ εἶμι) serves as the third singular imperfect ("would go off", as a matter of habit) of ἀπέρχομαι, cf. εἰσ-ῄει (twice) in §17, first person singular εἰσ-ῇα in §42, and the note on εἰσιών in §4.

καθευδήσουσα: Future participle expressing purpose, "to sleep".

ὡς: Here (cf. in §§18, 22, 23) a preposition with accus., "to (join) him", "to his side", after the leading verb ἀπιέναι; we might prefer to link it with καθ., "sleep by his side".

τιτθόν: "teat", "breast".

βοᾷ: Change of subject: <the child>; we might say "to stop the child ..."

ταῦτα ... οὕτως ἐγίγνετο: "things went on like this" (-ετο: neuter plural subject).

ἠλιθίως διεκείμην: On the verb see note on διακεῖσθαι in §3; ἠλίθιος means "silly, simple-minded": "I had such a naive way of looking at things".

ᾤμην i.e. ᾠόμην, from οἴεσθαι (cf. the very common οἶμαι, = οἴομαι, §§28, 35).

ἑαυτοῦ: Third person pronoun, here for ἐμαυτοῦ, a "normalising" variant reading here, "my own".

§11

προ-ϊόντος ... χρόνου: Genitive absolute, "time going forward": "time passed, <and this happened>:"; for -ιόντος see on εἰσιών in §4.

ἀγροῦ: "the country", where he will have had farm-property. The definite article is habitually suppressed with this noun.

ἐβόα ...: Imperfects, "started to ..."

ἐδυσκόλαινεν: This verb means "fret"; ~ adj. δύσκολος, "peevish, discontented".

ἵνα ...: Subject the child.

§12

ἀπ-ιέναι: Cf. on εἰσιών in §4.

ἐκέλευον: "issued instructions", very commonly employed in the imperfect.

τὸ .. πρῶτον: Adverbial, as often: "initially".

οὐκ ἤθελεν: "didn't want to" (and kept saying so), not "refused (outright)" (aorist).

ὡς ἄν (sometimes written ὡσάν) is a stereotyped way of saying "as if": "as though glad at having seen me ..."

ἑορακυῖα: On this perfect participle see *MS* A.3.b.

ἥκοντα: Often the element "back" can be mentally supplied with verbs of coming/going.

διὰ χρόνου: "after an interval of time", i.e. "after so long <away>".

ὠργιζόμην: Another inceptive imperfect, "began to ..."

ἵνα ...: "Yes [γε thus often; also emphasises pronoun here], <you're telling me to take my leave> so that *you* can <stay> here <and> try it on with your precious little slave-girl" (παιδίσκη, a diminutive of παῖς, here used contemptuously).

καὶ πρότερον δέ: "and [an indignant addition] on previous occasions also you were <seen to be> -ing ..." We gather that Euphiletus was not impotent or undersexed. He had fathered a child (§6) and he shared a bed with his wife (§10 init.).

εἷλκες: Imperfect of ἕλκειν (note the augment, cf. ἔχω ~ εἶχον), "draw, drag along", here "pull about", "paw".

§13

κἀγώ: καὶ ἐγώ.

ἐγέλων: Inceptive imperfect; his wife then enters into the spirit of things — or pretends to.

ἀνα-στᾶσα: ἀν-ιστάναι, "to make (somebody) stand up", intransitive in aorist participle -στάς -στᾶσα -στάν, "having stood up", "got to one's feet".

ἀπ-ιοῦσα: Present participle (cf. on εἰσιών in §4) because the departure is synchronous with the action described by the following verb.

προσ-τίθησι: "put to", in the sense "close, shut". On the tense of this verb and of ἐφέλκεται see on γίγνεται in §6.

τὴν κλεῖν ἐφέλκεται: κλεῖν is accusative of κλείς, "drew the <outside> bolt", locking in our poor innocent (now in the bedroom of what had been the women's quarters, secured from the outside).

οὐδέν: Adverbial (see Vocabulary for construction of ἐνθυμεῖσθαι).

ὑπο-νοῶν = ὑποπτεύων.

ἐκάθευδον: Imperfect, "proceeded to go to bed and get some sleep". Note the application of the augment to *a preverb* (καθ-εύδειν).

§14

πρός: "towards", "approaching".

ἀν-έῳξεν: On the augmentation cf. *MS* A.5.b.

ἐρομένου .. μου: Genitive absolute.

αἱ θύραι: Cf. on §17.

ψοφοῖεν: Optative: *MS* C.4.b.

ἀπο-σβεσθῆναι: From ἀπο-σβεννύναι, "to extinguish, put out".

ἐνάψασθαι: A middle of ἐν-άπτειν (ἅπτειν in the sense "set on fire, light"), "to get oneself/ procure a light" from the neighbours <' fire>. Cf. Homer *Odyssey* 5.488-90 (transl. W. Shewring) "A neighbourless man in some lonely spot will bury a burning log under grey ash, keeping alive the seed of fire and hoping thus not to need to rekindle it from elsewhere".

ἔδοξε: The speaker has kept his peace all this while and has been inclined to believe the story: but it did strike him (aorist!) that she was wearing make-up.

ἐψιμυθιῶσθαι: On the form of this perfect passive see *MS* A.5.b; ψιμυθιοῦν means "to apply to a surface ψιμύθιον, carbonate of lead", a substance used to whiten facial skin; τὸ πρόσωπον is accusative of respect.

τοῦ .. τεθνεῶτος: Genitive absolute; see on the participle *MS* A.3.a. In Athens thirty days was the period of mourning the death of a relative.

οὐδ' οὕτως οὐδὲν εἰπών: "not even in these circumstances saying nothing", a sequence of two negatives, one too many for English: "not even when faced with this did I pass any comment, but ..."

ἐξελθὼν ᾠχόμην ἔξω: οἴχεσθαι is commonly accompanied by a complementary participle expressing the notion "going": "I proceeded to go off out", the adverb ἔξω underlining the fact that he was not around long enough to allow his mind to be occupied with domestic matters.

§§15-21

Narrative, part two. Euphiletus gets wind of the liaison: a practised adulterer is at work, a story confirmed by the serving-girl who has been acting as go-between, and who must now arrange for Eratosthenes to be caught red-handed.

Vocabulary

Nouns

ὑποψία, ἡ	suspicion
ἐπιτήδειος, ὁ	close associate, intimate
ἐχθρός, ὁ	(personal) enemy
αἴτιον, τό	reason, cause
δωμάτιον, τό	bedroom
ἱερόν, τό	temple, shrine
πίστις, ἡ	pledge, assurance, guarantee
γόνυ -ατος, τό	knee (grasped in supplication)

Adjectives

κύριος	holding good, valid
μεστός	full (of, gen.)

Verbs

βασανίζειν	subject to (formal) interrogation (under torture)
ἀνα-μιμνῄσκεσθαι	recall, recollect
ἐκ-πλήττεσθαι	be struck out of <one's wits>, thunderstruck, astounded
ταράττεσθαι	be in turmoil
φοιτᾶν	visit regularly

κατ-ηγορεῖν	accuse (one, gen.), make an accusation (to the effect that, ὡς)
δεῖσθαι	need, require (with gen.; with acc./infin., that ...)
ἀξιοῦν	(with acc. person + infin.) demand, insist that one should
Adverbs	
ἐγγύς	near, in the vicinity; also with gen.
οἴκαδε	homewards, home

Aids to comprehension

§15

χρόνου ... ἀπολελειμμένου: Genitives absolute; the first literally "a period of time having intervened between-whiles" (cf. on διὰ χρόνου in §12), the second "me having been left at a great distance from [gen.] ..." (πολύ adverbial), i.e. "a (considerable) interval occurred during which I remained quite unaware of ..., when ..."

ἀπολελειμμένου: On the form of this participle see *MS* A.5.a.

προσέρχεται: Vivid present, cf. on γίγνεται in §6.

πρεσβῦτις ἄνθρωπος: "old female" (~ πρεσβύτης, "elderly man"), cf. ἡ ἄνθρωπος below and on ἀνθρώπου in §8.

ὑπο-πεμφθεῖσα: The force of the preverb is "secretly, on the quiet".

ἐμοίχευεν: See on ἐμοίχευεν in §4.

ὁμοίως: "in a similar fashion", i.e. "as he had done in the past".

ἕως with aorist indicative, "until" she (actually) discovered.

ὅ τι εἴη: "what was": on the optative see *MS* C.4.b.

§16

ἐγγύς ... τῆς οἰκίας together: the uncomplimentary ἡ ἄνθρωπος is interposed.

ἐπι-τηροῦσα: Cf. on §8.

μηδεμιᾷ πολυπραγμοσύνῃ is emphatically placed: "it isn't out of any meddlesomeness that I have ..., don't think that!" Cf. πολλὰ πράττειν, "be a(n interfering) busybody".

προσ-εληλυθέναι: Perfect infinitive of προσ-έρχομαι, see *MS* A.3.a.

ὢν ... τυγχάνει: τυγχ. with participle ("happen to be") can often bear the sense "be in (point of, actual) fact".

ἐὰν ...: Prospective conditional clause, cf. *MS* B.3.

διακονοῦσαν: -εῖν = "wait on" (~ διάκονος "servant, menial").

ὑμῖν plural: the household.

βασανίσῃς: There is no indication in the speech that Euphiletus offered to hand over the girl to his opponents for examination under torture (βάσανος), or that they demanded her for questioning. One possibility is that he had declined to take the latter course, and that the extended account offered here is making the point that a formal interrogation *had* been conducted, on his own terms and to his own satisfaction.

Ὀῆθεν: "from/ of <the deme> Oe".

διέφθαρκεν: Perfect: *MS* A.3.b.

ταύτην ... ἔχει: The bracketed τὴν (to indicate an interpolation), present in all manuscripts, would signify "because *this* is the trade he plies!". Without it (so most editors): "he practises this as a profession!" (for ταύτην cf. the note on §5).

§17

ἀπ-ηλλάγη: From ἀπ-αλλάττεσθαι, "be removed/ remove oneself", i.e. "take one's leave, make oneself scarce".

εὐθέως = εὐθύς.

γνώμην: "mind", or as we might prefer "head" (seat of reasoning faculty/ perception).

εἰσ-ῄει: Singular in conjunction with neuter plural subject; for the form cf. on ἀπῄει in §10.

ἀπ-εκλῄσθην: From ἀπο-κλείειν "shut up, away".

ἐψόφει: Singular because the two doors specified (the inside, viz. the door leading from ἀνδρωνῖτις into courtyard, αὐλή; and the outside, viz. the door leading from courtyard to street) can be naturally regarded as a single entity from the point of view of the observation about noise during the hours of darkness.

ὃ οὐδέποτε ἐγένετο: "a thing that had never happened in the past".

τε: "and", as already in §6.

ταῦτά μου ... γνώμην: μου with γνώμην (cf. above), the postpositive being slotted into the preferred second position in the sense-unit.

§18

ἐκέλευον ...: Euphiletus chooses not to have it out with his wife. Instead, he will tackle the go-between. Since this cannot be done indoors, the unsuspecting girl is told to accompany her master on a shopping-trip. In keeping with his mission to uphold civic justice, the aggrieved husband is now made to behave like a stern but responsible official at an inquest.

ὡς: Preposition with accusative, "to <the home of> one of ..."

εἴην πεπυσμένος: For the form and employment of this perfect optative see *MS* A.4/ C.4.a.

δυοῖν ὁπότερον: "whichever of two courses" (ὁπότερος: cf. οὐδέτερος, "neither of two"; δυοῖν is genitive of δύο).

μαστιγωθεῖσαν ...: The accusative and infinitive construction is now brought into play: "to be whipped [μαστιγοῦν ~ μάστιξ "whip"] and pitched into a mill". μύλων: hard labour in the mill was a punishment for slaves.

ἐμ-πεσεῖν: πίπτειν "fall", often "be thrown".

συν-εχομένην: This compound means "be held together", hence "constrained, afflicted, oppressed".

κατ-ειποῦσαν: κατ-ειπεῖν = "declare", "divulge" information.

τἀληθῆ: τὰ ἀληθῆ.

τυχεῖν: Cf. on τυγχάνειν in §2.

τῶν ἡμαρτημένων: Genitive of τὰ ἡμαρτημένα, cf. *MS* A.5.b; pardon of = pardon for.

ψεύσῃ .. μηδέν: A stern prohibition, see *MS* B.5.

§§19-20

κἀκείνη: καὶ ἐκείνη.

ἔξαρνος (two-termination adjective): "denying", with ἦν, a slightly more formal way of saying ἐξ-ηρνεῖτο (ἐξ-αρνεῖσθαι, "to deny").

... βούλομαι: The tense reflects that of the original declaration.

εἰδέναι: "<she said> that she knew", the verb of saying to be extracted from the preceding "instructed". On the perfect infinitive see *MS* A.2.a.

ἐμνήσθην: Aorist of μιμνήσκεσθαι, in the sense "mention", with genitive.

εἴη: See on the optative *MS* C.4.a.

ἡγησαμένη: "having considered", i.e. "since now she had come round to believing".

ἐγνωκέναι: Perfect infinitive of γιγνώσκειν, *MS* A.3.b; "to have come to know, be in the picture about".

τότε ἤδη: "then right away", "there and then".

πεσοῦσα: "throwing herself", cf. on ἐμπεσεῖν in §18.

πείσεσθαι: Future infinitive (a pledge "that she would ...") of πάσχειν.

προσίοι/ εἰσαγγείλειε/ πεισθείη/ προσίοιτο: On this string of optatives see the remarks in *MS* C.4.a.

προσ-ίοι: προσ-ιέναι, cf. on εἰσιών in §4.

ἔπειτα: "in the next place", with δέ suppressed, as so often (cf. εἶτα in §40).

τελευτῶσα: "finishing off", a common personal construction for which we substitute adverbial "finally", "ultimately".

τῷ χρόνῳ: "in time", "in due course".

καὶ τὰς ... προσ-ίοιτο (middle of προσ-ιέναι i.e. προσ-ίημι): Literally "and the entries by what methods she was in the habit of admitting", that is to say, "and as for his <various> entries <into the speaker's house>, <she described> the methods she employed to effect them".

Θεσμοφορίοις: The dative means "at, on the occasion of" the festival Thesmophoria. Cf. on §8 (funeral).

ἐμοῦ ... ὄντος: Genitive absolute.

μητρός: Euphiletus is concerned about the way adulterers disrupt family unity. His wife is in with her lover's mother as well.

τἆλλα: τὰ ἄλλα.

§21

εἴρητο: A third singular (neuter plural subject) pluperfect, see *MS* A.6.

αὐτῇ: The dative is the normal way of expressing the personal agent ("by") with perfect/ pluperfect.

ὅπως ... πεύσεται: ὅπως μή with future indicative in issuing a solemn warning: "Right then, just you make sure that not a single soul gets wind of <all> this!".

εἰ δὲ μή: A stereotyped way (cf. in §§36, 48) of saying "otherwise".

τῶν ... ὡμολογημένων: Genitive of τὰ ὡμολογημένα, see *MS* A.5.b.

ἐπ' αὐτοφώρῳ: Common in the sense "in the very act".

δέομαι: A switch here from genitive to accusative and infinitive, see introductory Vocabulary to §15-21.

εἴ-περ: "if really", "if in fact".

ποιήσειν: Future infinitive, since implementation of the agreement is prospective: in English "that she would do" or just "to do".

§§22-28

Narrative, part three. Things come to a head when Euphiletus is told of Eratosthenes' presence in the house. He sets off to gather all the witnesses he can track down, bursts into the bedroom and dispatches the wrongdoer, after rejecting an offer of monetary compensation, with an appeal to "the law of the polis". The charge of entrapment is firmly rejected, as is the assertion that the killing was carried out at the sacred household hearth.

Vocabulary

Nouns

ἑστία, ἡ	hearth
κλίνη, ἡ	couch, bed
ἀργύριον, τό	(sum of) money
τεκμήριον, τό	proof, (item of) evidence; plur. (body of) evidence

Adjectives

κόσμιος	decently behaved, law-abiding
τελευταῖος	last, final

Verbs

ἀνα-γιγνώσκειν	read out
ἐπ-εγείρειν	wake up, rouse
ἱκετεύειν	supplicate, beseech
κατα-λαμβάνειν	catch, find
κατα-φεύγειν	flee for refuge, protection
παρα-βαίνειν	transgress, offend against
παρα-λαμβάνειν	take along
πατάσσειν	strike (one) a blow
πλήττειν	strike, hit
φράζειν	tell, explain
ἀμύνεσθαι	repulse, repel
ἀπ-αντᾶν	(with dative) meet, encounter
μηχανᾶσθαι	contrive, cook up
ἀντι-βολεῖν	supplicate, implore
ἐπι-δημεῖν	be in town (Athens)
(συν)δειπνεῖν	have dinner (with one)
ὠθεῖν	shove, push (open)
ἐπι-μελεῖσθαι	(with gen.) look after, attend to

Adverbs

οἴκοι	at home
ὄπισθεν	behind, at the rear
τηνικαῦτα	at that (particular) time

Aids to comprehension

§22

διεγένοντο: "there occurred an interval of", cf. on §15 ad init.

ὡς ["as"] ἐγὼ ...: Clearly something has dropped out of the text before this declaration, along the lines of "and I did in fact catch the fellow red-handed".

μεγάλοις: "strong", "compelling".

... ἡμέρᾳ: Dative marking a point in time, "on ..."

Σώστρατος ... τούτῳ ...: A businesslike start: no connecting particles as the speaker embarks on his account of events. For Sostratus, who must have been a key witness in the case, see §§39-40.

ἡλίου δεδυκότος: Genitive absolute; on the perfect, "to have set", see *MS* A.3.a.

ἰόντι: Cf. on εἰσιών in §4.

εἰδώς: *MS* A.2.a.

ἀφιγμένος: Perfect participle of ἀφικνεῖσθαι, *MS* A.4.

οὐδέν: The οὐδὲν ἂν of the manuscripts has often been corrected to οὐδένα: but "none of his close circle/ those close to him" reads very oddly indeed. With οὐδέν alone we can translate "none of the necessities" (a neuter plural), i.e. "no provisions at all" — nothing on the menu at this late hour for his main meal of the day. The unacceptable ἄν will have arisen from a misunderstanding of the function of the ensuing optative.

κατα-λήψοιτο: Future optative of -λαμβάνειν (future infinitive -λήψεσθαι), cf. *MS* C.4.a.

ὡς: Preposition with accusative once again.

ἀνα-βάντες: From ἀνα-βαίνειν (aorist participle -βάς -βᾶσα -βάν), "having ascended", "gone upstairs".

ὑπερῷον: "room on the upper level", where the ἀνδρωνῖτις was temporarily.

§23

ἐπειδὴ ... εἶχεν: Literally "when it was well for him", i.e. "after enjoying a good/ proper meal" — the reason for the invitation; καλῶς ἔχει μοι means "I'm fine", "I'm happy with what I've had".

εἶχεν: Augmentation: cf. on εἷλκες in §12.

ἀπ-ιὼν ᾤχετο: See on εἰσιών in §4 and on ᾠχόμην in §14.

ἐκάθευδον: "I went to bed", cf. on §13 ad fin.

εἰσέρχεται and φράζει: Further examples of the "historic present" (4 more cases in §§23-25), cf. on γίγνεται in §6.

ἐστί: Present representing the tense in which the original utterance will have been cast, cf. ὑβρίζει in §25.

κἀγώ: καὶ ἐγώ.

εἰπών: Here "telling" = "instructing".

κατα-βάς: Cf. on ἀνα-βάντες in §22.

ὡς τὸν καὶ τόν: The τόνs here have the force of demonstratives (as in ὁ μέν/ ὁ δέ, cf. below), "to <the home of> one, then another".

<οὐκ>: Angular brackets indicate an insertion — this an inescapable one — by modern editors.

οὐδ' corrected from οὐκ: "not even".

§24

ὡς ... πλείστους: ὡς with superlative can itself mean "as ... as possible" (cf. in §42).

ἐβάδιζον: "I proceeded <homewards>".

δᾷδας: δᾴς gen. δᾳδός, ἡ = "torch" (uncontracted form: δαΐς: ~ δαίειν "kindle").

τοῦ ἐγγύτατα καπηλείου: "from the nearest shop"; we can represent the adverb (superlative, alternative form ἐγγυτάτω in §41: positive ἐγγύς) as an adjective. καπηλεῖον: the establishment of a κάπηλος, a retail tradesman.

ἀνεῳγμένης ...: Genitive absolute; on the perfect participles see *MS* A.5.b.

εἰσ-ιόντες: Cf. on εἰσιών in §4.

ἔτι with κατακείμενον, drawn forward to emphasise the point that Eratosthenes was indeed caught "in the act".

κατα-κείμενον: "lying down", cf. *MS* A.2.b.

οἱ δ' ὕστερον: Supply εἰσιόντες.

ἑστηκότα: See *MS* A.3.b.

§25

τὼ χεῖρε: Accusative dual of ἡ χείρ, "both his hands".

περι-αγαγὼν εἰς τοὔπισθεν (~ τὸ ὄπισθεν) i.e. "having drawn ... behind his back".

δήσας: ἔδησα is aorist of δεῖν = "tie up".

ὑβρίζει ... εἰσιών recalls the charge levelled in the prooemium, §4 (cf. also ὕβριν in §2).

εἰσ-ιών: Cf. on εἰσιών in §4.

κἀκεῖνος: καὶ ἐκεῖνος.

ἀδικεῖν .. ὡμολόγει: "admitted that he was guilty/ his guilt".

ἠντεβόλει: Note the double augment.

πράξασθαι: Middle in the sense "exact for oneself", "negotiate a settlement" in the form of a sum of money. Not surprisingly, there is no mention of a course open (and, one would have thought, attractive) to an aggrieved party with witnesses, that of taking the offender to court on a charge of μοιχεία.

§26

The bedroom is now, somewhat implausibly, turned into a court of law, with a dignified Euphiletus presiding — and deciding on the spot what is to be done.

ὅτι "that" often prefaces *direct* speech.

περὶ ἐλάττονος ... ἐποιήσω: Cf. on περὶ πολλοῦ ποιεῖσθαι in §1: "rate less highly", "regard as less important" than ...

ἁμάρτημα ἐξαμαρτάνειν strikes a solemn note; Greek is of course fond of such pairings: μάχην μάχεσθαι, νίκην νικᾶν etc. etc. Cf. in §44 (twice, see note), §45.

εἰς γυναῖκα ...: Cf. in §4: here however, in the context of the slaying, there is no mention of the outrage done to his own person.

§27

ὧνπερ ... κελεύουσι: Supply τυχεῖν (with genitive = "receive, get"): i.e. the precise (form of) punishment that ..., cf. on -περ in §1.

εἰσ-αρπασθείς: "snatched and dragged into <the house>" after being enticed there by the slave girl.

οὗτοι: The relatives bringing the prosecution.

πῶς .. ἄν; "how could <he have done so>?".

ὅστις: Sometimes, like the ordinary relative ὅς, causal: "because here was a person who ..."
περι-έστρεψα: "turned, twisted round", i.e. "pinned behind him".
οὓς: "so many whom" amounts to "so many that ... them".
δια-φυγεῖν: "slip through" to make a getaway.
σίδηρον .. ξύλον: "an object made of iron or of wood".

§28

οἶμαι: Cf. on ᾤμην in §10.
καί i.e. as well as I do.
εἰδέναι: Cf. *MS* A.2.a.
οἱ μὴ ...: As the negative (μή not οὐ) indicates, generic: "people who do not ..."
τὰ τοιαῦτα μηχανώμενοι: "by resorting to such tricks".
ὀργὰς ... παρα-σκευάζουσι: "contrive to stir up angry reactions" among.
κατά with genitive, "against".
ἀνά-γνωθι: Singular aorist imperative, addressed to the clerk.
ΝΟΜΟΣ: None of the documents or depositions specified has survived. At this point a clause from the νόμος μοιχείας relating to the course of action taken by Euphiletus must have been read out: cf. introductory note to speech.

§§29-31

Eratosthenes admitted his guilt and was punished in accordance with "the law of the polis", one with the authority of the Areopagus behind it. A comparison of the treatment accorded to those caught with (a) married women and (b) concubines.

Vocabulary

Nouns

γαμετή (γυνή)	married woman
παλλακή, ἡ	concubine, mistress
φόνος, ὁ	homicide
δικαστήριον, τό	court of law
δάμαρ -αρτος, ἡ	wife
μάρτυς -υρος, ὁ	witness
Adjectives	
ἕτοιμος	ready, prepared (to, infin.)
ἰσχυρός	strong, severe
Verbs	
ἀπο-τίνειν	pay in compensation
κατα-γιγνώσκειν	convict (one, gen.) of (an offence, acc.)
τάττειν	prescribe, stipulate

ἀμφισ-βητεῖν	dispute a point
συγ-χωρεῖν	agree with, accede to (dat.)
ἐπι-τιθέναι	impose upon (dat.)
Adverb	
σφόδρα	strongly, vehemently
Particle	
καίτοι	(and) yet

Aids to comprehension

§29

ἠμφεσβήτει: Cf. the note on ἠντεβόλει in §25.

ὅπως .. μὴ ...: See on the construction *MS* B.2.c.

τιμήματι: "assessment", his personal "estimate" as offender of the penalty to be imposed.

εἶναι κυριώτερον: "(insisted that ... should) have greater authority".

ταύτην ... δίκην: "I exacted that penalty". The details of the killing are suppressed.

ἡγησάμενοι: Best represented by a principal verb: "*you* considered ... when you prescribed ..."

μοι: "for me", "in response to me", a common way of saying "please".

ΜΑΡΤΥΡΕΣ: There to confirm the story of what happened on the night of the killing.

§30

ἐκ ... ἐξ: We would say "from the pillar *on* the Areopagus".

ᾧ ... δικάζειν: "for which it is (which enjoys) an ancestral right, and <to which> no less in our day the <same> right has been granted, <I mean the right> to judge cases of homicide". πάτριος: lit. "relating to one's πατέρες, fathers/ forefathers"; ἐπί with genitive is common in the sense "in the time of".

ἀποδέδοται: Cf. on §2.

διαρρήδην: "expressly", "categorically".

εἴρηται: Perfect passive (*MS* A.5.b), hence the preceding dative of agent δικαστηρίῳ, cf. on αὐτῇ in §21.

ὃς ἂν ... + subjunctive: see *MS* B.4.

ἐπί: "with regard to", "in the case of": so recurrently in what follows.

ποιήσηται: "has manufactured for himself", i.e. "has taken it upon himself to exact" this <particular form of> punishment.

§31

νομοθέτης: "framer of a/ the law", "lawgiver": ~ νόμον τιθέναι "enact a law" (cf. in §§33, 48).

ὥστε καί: "that he actually/ even": καί often reinforces ὥστε with (emphatic) indicative.

παλλακαῖς: Not any concubine (as the argument might suggest) but freeborn concubines, whether Athenian or foreign, taken "with a view to fathering free children" (Demosthenes 23.53).

ἐλάττονος: "of less <consideration, regard>".

εἶχε not ἔσχε: "had at his disposal" in deciding the issue.

ταύτης: Genitive of comparison; another example follows.

μείζω: Irregular comparative of μέγας; accusative singular, alternative form μείζονα.

ἐποίησεν: Cf. ποιήσηται above: "put into effect, bring into force".

νῦν δέ (as often) "but as things stood", "but as it was".

τὴν αὐτὴν καὶ ἐπὶ ...: καί often means "as" in conjunction with words denoting "the same": "the same mode of punishment as <obtained> in the case of ..."

ΝΟΜΟΣ: The law dealing with rape.

§§32-36

Observations on the penalties imposed on rapists and seducers. The former are dealt with less harshly than the latter, since seduction involves destruction of a household's harmony and integrity. For this reason Euphiletus has been commanded by the laws to take drastic action. It is the jury's responsibility to deter would-be adulterers.

Vocabulary

Nouns	
ψῆφος, ἡ	vote
κλέπτης, ὁ	thief, burglar
Adjectives	
ἀλλότριος	belonging to other people
οἰκεῖος	(with dat.) attached (to), on intimate terms (with)
Verbs	
ἀπο-γιγνώσκειν	acquit (construction: see below)
ὀφείλειν	owe, have to pay
ἅπτεσθαι	(with gen.) touch, lay hands on
βιάζεσθαι	apply force, act violently
δια-πράττεσθαι	achieve one's ends
παρα-κελεύεσθαι	(with dat.) urge
ἀπορεῖν	be at a loss, perplexed (about, acc.)
μισεῖν	hate

Aids to comprehension

§§32-33

κελεύει: Subject the νομοθέτης.

ἐάν clauses: see *MS* B.3.

ἄνθρωπον ... παῖδα: "a free-born male adult or minor".

αἰσχύνῃ βίᾳ: "forcibly shames", i.e. rapes.

διπλῆν τὴν βλάβην: "double the damages <due for raping a slave>", the latter penalty presumably having been specified in the preceding ΝΟΜΟΣ.

γυναῖκα, ἐφ' αἷσπερ ...: "a woman, in the case of which particular [-περ] category [a switch to the plural, harking back to the case of *seduced* women, so highlighting the less severe penalty dealt out to *rapists*] it is permissible to exact the death-penalty" (this verb often has the sense "put to death, execute").

ἐν ... ἐν-έχεσθαι: "to be held in the same things" means "to be subject/ liable to the selfsame penalty". — Things were not as straightforward as this observation suggests. It was almost certainly the case that the law in question also exempted from condemnation for murder a man who killed someone caught in the act of *raping* his wife, mother, sister, daughter or free mistress. Since Euphiletus is out to prove that seduction is a far more serious offence than rape, he does not refer to this. It is also exceedingly likely that rapists could be prosecuted on grounds of ὕβρις, a process whereby the successful prosecutor could propose any penalty he wished, including capital punishment.

τοὺς βιαζομένους ... τοὺς πείθοντας: "those who employ force [= rapists] ... those who use persuasion [= seducers]"; τῶν = seducers, τοῖς = rapists.

τῶν βιασθέντων: "those upon whom force has been employed".

αὑτοῖς: n.b. αὑ- not αὐ-, "themselves".

πᾶσαν ... γεγονέναι: Note the change of subject; ἐπ' + dative here means "under the control of", "in the power of"; perfect infinitive γεγονέναι (*MS* A.3.a) = "to have become", "to come for good".

τοὺς παῖδας ... ὄντες: "the children are unclear (i.e., as for the children, it is unclear) to which of the two parties they actually belong". For ὁποτέρων cf. on §18; for τυγχάνειν, on §16.

ἀνθ' [= ἀντί] ὧν: "for which/ these reasons".

τιθείς: Cf. on νομοθέτης in §31.

§34

ἀπεγνωκότες εἰσὶ ... κεκελευκότες: On the periphrastic perfects see *MS* A.3.a-b; ἀπο-γιγνώσκειν with gen. person and μή + infinitive means "acquit one of *doing*", μή simply strengthening the element of negation present in the leading verb.

ἐν ὑμῖν ... πότερον i.e. in your hands/ for you to decide whether ...

ἰσχυρούς: "strong", here in the sense "effective", "valid".

§35

μέν: There is no answering δέ. This is often the case when μέν is associated with words expressing opinion, "implicitly contrasted with certainty or reality" as J.D. Denniston puts it (*The Greek Particles* 382).

οἶμαι: Cf. on ᾤμην in §10.

διὰ τοῦτο: Note the position: "that it is for this reason/ with this in mind that ..."

τίθεσθαι: Middle this time: "make/ frame their laws".

ἵνα ... σκεψώμεθα: Two subjunctive-clauses, one final, one indefinite: see *MS* B.2.a/ B.4.

ὧν: Relative attraction, i.e. τούτων τῶν πραγμάτων, ἃ ἂν (πράγματα) ἀπορῶμεν, the substantival antecedent being drawn into the actual relative clause.

παρά: "to" them, as if paying them a visit for a consultation.

ποιητέον: A verbal adjective, literally "what is necessary-to be-done by us": *dative* of agent, as commonly with the -τέος type; cf. too the note on αὐτῇ in §21.

οὗτοι: Emphatic: "it is *these* ... which ..."

§36

οἷς ... τὴν αὐτὴν γνώμην ἔχειν: Relative again (cf. in §33) serving as sentence-connective: "the same opinion as these/ they hold" (compendiously for "as <the opinion of> these"; cf. on τῶν αὐτῶν in §2). As the jurors had sworn an oath to abide by the laws of the assembly they could not but concur with what the laws prescribe.

εἰ δὲ μή: Cf. on §21.

ἄδειαν ... ποιήσετε: "create/ afford ... legal immunity" (ἄδεια = "freedom from fear" [~ adj. ἀδεής], "safe conduct").

ὥστε καί: Cf. on §31.

κλέπτας: Under Athenian law thieves caught red-handed at night could be killed by the victim.

ἐπ-αρεῖτε: ἐπ-αίρειν = "induce, incite".

εἰδότας: Cf. *MS* A.2.a.

ἐάν clause: *MS* B.3.

ἐπὶ τούτῳ: "for this purpose".

εἰσ-ιέναι: Cf. the note on εἰσιών in §4.

χαίρειν ἐᾶν: "to allow to rejoice" (but recall too χαῖρε, "farewell") is a common way of saying "to disregard, dismiss, forget about, write off".

τὴν ... δεδιέναι: "whereas it is *your* vote that they have to fear". On the perfect infinitive see *MS* A.3.a.

αὕτη ... κυριωτάτη: "because it is this that has supreme authority over all affairs of state".

§§37-42

While maintaining that any *mode of redress would be justifiable in the circumstances, Euphiletus refutes the claim that he had resorted to enticement in order to get his hands on Eratosthenes. Premeditation must be ruled out in the light of Sostratus' involvement and other considerations.*

Vocabulary

Nouns

νεανίσκος, ὁ	young man/ fellow
θεράπων -οντος, ὁ	servant
Adjective	
ἔρημος	solitary, abandoned, isolated
Verbs	
ἐπι-βουλεύειν	(with dat.) plot against, set a trap for
παρ-αγγέλλειν	transmit messages, send word to (dat.)
περι-τρέχειν	run around, here there and everywhere
συλ-λέγεσθαι	(be) gather(ed), assemble
τολμᾶν	dare
σωφρονεῖν	act reasonably, exercise proper self-control

Aids to comprehension

§37-38

γάρ: Cf. on γάρ in §6.

μετ-ελθεῖν: "to go and fetch", "seek out".

... ἂν .. ἡγούμην: ἄν with imperfect, "would be considering", "would consider": the speaker mentally recreates his thoughts and actions at that time; cf. ἠδίκουν ἄν ("would be guilty") in §38, <ἂν> ... ἡγούμην ibid.; and the cast of the sentence εἰ ἐν ... εἰσαγαγεῖν in §40.

ᾡτινιοῦν τρόπῳ: ᾡτινιοῦν is dative singular of ὁστισ-οῦν, "who(so)ever": "by any method whatsoever", "by any means available to me".

λαμβάνων: The present participle expresses the idea "in attempting/ seeking to catch", cf. the imperfect ἐλάμβανον presently.

λόγων ... εἰσεληλυθότος: Genitives absolute; the first two perfect participles (*MS* A.5.b/ A.5.a) express a condition, "if ..." (note negative μηδενός); the second pair (*MS* A.5.a/ A.3.a), introduced by the temporal adverb ἤδη, may be translated "once ... had ...."

δια-πεπραγμένων puts the middle δια-πράττεσθαι, "achieve his objectives", into passive form.

§39

ταῦτα ψεύδονται: "are telling lies in respect of these things", "about this".

γνώσεσθε: Future of γιγνώσκειν, "realise".

ὅπερ ...: Translate "just as ... in fact".

οἰκείως διακείμενος: "on intimate terms with me": cf. on διακεῖσθαι in §3.

δυσμάς: δυσμαί, "setting", usually in the plural, like its antonym, ἀν(α)τολαί.

καλῶς ... ᾤχετο: Cf. on §23.

§40

[ὅτι]: There is no place for "that" — an insertion made without regard for the following disjunction πότερον ... ἤ.

πότερον "whether" often prefaces a *direct* question — redundant in English.

κρεῖττον: "better", "more advantageous" for me to dine elsewhere myself, or to bring into the house (εἰσ-) ...

τὸν συνδειπνήσοντά μοι: Future participle with article, "the one going to have dinner with me", that is to say, "somebody to have ..."

οὕτω: "in these circumstances", i.e. "in the latter eventuality".

... ἂν ἧττον ἐτόλμησεν: "would have been less inclined to dare/ take a chance on ..."

εἶτα to mark the next step in the argument, "then again", picking up πρῶτον μέν (cf. on §20); another stab with ἔπειτα, §41 init.

δοκῶ ἂν ὑμῖν ... καταλειφθῆναι: "do I seem would to you ... to have been left behind?", i.e. "do you think that I would have been left behind?", postpositive ἄν being drawn forward to second place in the sense-unit. In negative form in §41, "not would I seem to you to have ...?", = "don't you think I would have ...?" (cf. in §42).

ἀφείς: Aorist participle of ἀφ-ιέναι ~ ἀφ-ίημι, "let go, dismiss".

ἵνα ... ἐτιμωρεῖτο: "so that he might punish". ἵνα with indicative: the imperfect (aorist or pluperfect if the reference is to past time) is employed in cases where the action of the main verb is not fulfilled, so that the purpose is not achievable. Cf. εἰσῇα and ἐποιούμην in §42.

§41

μεθ' ἡμέραν: "by day", "in the daytime".

τὴν ἐγγυτάτω: "<I mean, naturally,> the one nearest <to my own>".

ἐπειδὴ τάχιστα: "as soon as", "the moment that".

τῆς νυκτός: Genitive of time within which something occurs, "in the night", "during the night hours".

εἰδώς (again in §42): Cf. *MS* A.2.a.

καταλήψομαι: The future tense carries us back in time to the problem as it presented itself to the speaker on the night in question.

καὶ ...: "and in fact I did go to <the home> of ..."
τὸν δεῖνα: ὁ δεῖνα = "so and so": "to somebody else's".
ᾔδη: Past tense of οἶδα, cf. in §42, and *MS* A.2.a.

§42

καίτοι γε ...: "yet/ but surely, if I did have foreknowledge".
καὶ ... καί: "both ... and".
παρασκευάσασθαι: Middle in the sense "prepare/ provide for one's own use", "arrange for them to be there at the ready".
ἵν' ... εἰσῇα ... ἐποιούμην: Cf. on §40 above, and for the form -ῇα the note on ἀπῄει in §10.
ὡς ἀσφαλέστατα ... ὡς .. πλείστων: See on §24 ad init.
τί .. ᾔδη: "in what respect did I know?", i.e. "how could I have known?".
κἀκεῖνος: καὶ ἐκεῖνος; καί = "as well" as the speaker.
σιδήριον (cf. in §27): "iron tool" etc., here "weapon with a blade", "knife".
ὡς μετὰ πλείστων δὲ μαρτύρων: In prepositional phrases involving ὡς, "as ... as possible", that word comes first; and δέ is commonly postponed when used in conjunction with preposition + adjective or pronoun or noun.
νῦν δ': Cf. on §31.
τῶν ἐσομένων: Genitive of τὰ ἐσόμενα, future participle of εἶναι, "of what was going to happen".

§§43-50

Amplification of the denial of any personal animosity between the two men (cf. in §4), restatement of the enormity of the crime (cf. in §2), refutation of any act of impiety (cf. in §27), reflections on the crucial part played by a right-minded jury and on the absurdities of permissive legislation (cf. in §36), with a final reminder that the speaker is risking all because he obeyed "the laws of the polis" (cf. in §§26, 29).

Vocabulary

Nouns

λοιδορία, ἡ	abuse, insulting language
ἀγών -ῶνος, ὁ	competition; legal action, trial
ἔνιοι	some people/ individuals

Adjective

ἴδιος	personal, private

Verbs

ἐκ-βάλλειν	throw out, expel, banish
ἀσεβεῖν	act impiously

ἐπι-θυμεῖν	be eager, anxious, desire
ἐπι-χειρεῖν	attempt
ζητεῖν	enquire, look into a question
παρα-καλεῖν	summon
ζημιοῦν	penalise
συν-ειδέναι	be aware of, privy to

Aids to comprehension

§43

ἀκηκόατε/ γεγένηται: See *MS* A.3.a/ A.5.a.
παρ' ὑμῖν αὐτοῖς: "before yourselves" <as judges>, i.e. "in your own minds".

§44

συκοφαντῶν: -εῖν = "play the part of a συκοφάντης", a professional informer/ prosecutor who sets out to "get" people by bringing (in the perception of the victim) baseless charges out of malicious and self-seeking motives.
γραφάς .. ἐγράψατο ~ ἰδίας δίκας ἐδικάζετο: Note the alternation of tenses: "he had neither brought state-prosecutions against me [γράφεσθαι = "indict" for some public offence] ... nor did he make any move to engage in private lawsuits". On the linkage of verb with cognate noun (cf. in §45, twice) see the note on ἁμάρτημα ἐξαμαρτάνειν in §26.
συν-ῄδει: *MS* A.2.a.
κακόν: "criminal act, misdemeanour".
δεδιὼς μή ...: Cf. *MS* A.3.a/ B.2.b; i.e. "... of which I was afraid, in case ..., so desiring ..."
οὔτε εἰ ...: "nor, if [cf. *MS* C.2.b] I were to have carried this out [his destruction], was I entertaining hopes of ... -ing ..."
ποθεν: Unaccented, indefinite: "from anywhere, some quarter".
λήψεσθαι ~ λαμβάνειν, "to get", future infinitive dependent on ἐλπίζειν.

§45

τοσούτου ... ἦ: Literally (δεῖν with genitive, "miss, need, require"), "λοιδορία ... lacks so much to have taken place for us that ...", i.e. "so far from any abusive exchange or drunken quarrel or any other sort of difference [cf. δια-φέρεσθαι, "be at variance"] having arisen between us, I had never as much as laid eyes on ..."
γεγονέναι: *MS* A.3.a.
ἑορακὼς ἦ: On the periphrastic pluperfect (another shortly: ἦ ... ἠδικημένος) see *MS* A.6.
τί ... βουλόμενος: "what wishing ...?", i.e. "what would be my motive in running such a risk?"

ἄν with ἐκινδύνευον (tense: see note on ἄν .. ἡγούμην in §§37-38), cf. on δοκῶ ἂν ὑμῖν ... in §40.

τὸ μέγιστον ... ἢ ... ἠδικημένος: One can say ἀδικίαν or ἀδίκημα ἀδικεῖν, "inflict a wrong"; this can be converted into the passive, "have a wrong inflicted on one", thus: ἀδικίαν/ ἀδίκημα ἀδικεῖσθαι.

§46

ἔπειτα: Cf. on §§20, 40.

παρακαλέσας ... ἠσέβουν: There is no ἄν this time, nor is one to be mentally supplied: "did I <really> take the step myself of summoning witnesses and *then* proceed to commit an act of impiety?".

ἐξόν: *Impersonal* ἔξ-εστι, "it is possible, permissible", hence *accusative* absolute: "when it was open to me ... that none should (to have nobody) ...".

εἴπερ: "if really/ genuinely", cf. in §21.

συν-ειδέναι: *MS* A.2.a.

§47

οἷα ...: Cuttingly: "the nature of [cf. on οἷοι in §1] the prizes/ the kind of prizes that are set up for ..."; προ-κεῖσθαι, "to have been placed before one", on open display; see *MS* A.2.b.

ἧττον: See on §40.

ἐάν clause: *MS* B.3.

§48

εἰ δὲ μή: Cf. on §21.

πολύ: Adverbial, "far"; again in §49.

κειμένους: "that have been set up/ framed", i.e. "established"; serving as perfect passive participle (cf. *MS* A.2.b) of τιθέναι: cf. θεῖναι presently, and see the comment on νομοθέτης in §31.

ἐξ-αλεῖψαι: Strong language: ἐξ-αλείφειν = "wipe out/ clean, obliterate".

οἵτινες ... ζημιώσουσι: A regular way of expressing purpose, "ones which will/ to ..."

§49

ἢ ... ἐν-εδρεύεσθαι: "that the citizen-body should be ensnared" (~ ἐν-έδρα, "sitting in", "ambush"), an interesting choice of metaphor given the suspicion of entrapment attaching to this case.

ἐάν τις ...: Cf. *MS* B.3.

ὅ τι ἂν οὖν βούληται: See *MS* B.4, and the note on ῴτινιοῦν in §37-38: "(in respect of ~) in whatever way he wants".

χρῆσθαι: "to use" = "to treat" a person.

οἱ δ' ...: After "the laws stipulate μέν that ..." we do not expect the sentence to take the turn it does; so the speaker puts his point across all the more forcefully.
ἀγῶνες: See the Vocabulary; echoes the imagery of prizes in §47.
δεινότεροι: "more threatening, dangerous".
καθ-εστήκασιν: On this perfect see *MS* A.3.b; intransitive, "have established themselves as", "have come to be".
παρά: "in contravention of", "contrary to", opp. κατὰ τοὺς νόμους (cf. in §4).
καταισχύνουσι: Dative participle.

§50
καὶ περὶ ...: Emphatic repetition to produce a forceful close.
σώματος: "body" for "life".

SUGGESTIONS FOR FURTHER READING

M. Edwards, referred to at the beginning of the Notes, provides a wide-ranging bibliography. The following two editions are extremely useful in different ways:

Carey, C., *Lysias: Selected Speeches* (Cambridge, 1989)

Edwards, M. and Usher, S., *Greek Orators I: Antiphon and Lysias* (Warminster, 1985).

Cf. too:

Fisher, N.R.E., *Social Values in Classical Athens* (London, 1976), esp. pp. 46-53.

Recent studies include:

Carey, C., 'Rape and Adultery in Athenian Law', *Classical Quarterly* n.s. 45 (1995) 407-17.

Harris, E.M., 'Did the Athenians Regard Seduction as a Worse Crime than Rape?', id. n.s. 40 (1990) 370-7.

Herman, G. 'Tribal and Civic Codes of Behaviour in Lysias i', id. n.s. 43 (1993) 406-19.

APPENDIX A
SURVEY OF VERBAL FORMS

If you have mastered the Greek verbal systems you will not need to consult this review of those forms which actually occur in the speech (with the exception of perfect/ pluperfect, dealt with elsewhere); if you have not, you might find it profitable to run through these pages with a full set of paradigms (available in any course-book or grammar) by your side. You should make a point of consulting the alphabetical key in Appendix B in cases of difficulty.

A.1 Infinitive in -ειν

Present infinitive ἁμαρτάνειν ἀποκτείνειν etc. (18 examples in all)
Present indicative 1st singular καταβάλλω κινδυνεύω νομίζω, 3rd singular ἔχει κελεύει τυγχάνει ὑβρίζει φράζει, 2nd plural ἀκούετε, 3rd plural ἐπιβουλεύουσι κελεύουσι λέγουσι παρασκευάζουσι τυγχάνουσιν
Present subjunctive 3rd singular αἰσχύνῃ ἐθέλῃ κινδυνεύῃ, 3rd plural λέγωσι φάσκωσιν
Present optative 2nd plural ἔχοιτε
Present imperative singular λέγε νόμιζε
Present participle masculine ἔχων ἥκων λαμβάνων λέγων μεθύων παραβαίνων παραλείπων πράττων προσφέρων ὑβρίζων; ἥκοντα; πράττοντες; ἔχοντας πείθοντας πράττοντας φυλάττοντας; ἐπιτηδευόντων πραττόντων; ἀκούουσι ἐπιτηδεύουσιν καταισχύνουσι — feminine καταβαίνουσα νομίζουσα; βαδίζουσαν — neuter ἔχον κλᾶον

Imperfect with syllabic augment 1st singular ἐβάδιζον ἐκέλευον ἐκινδύνευον ἐλάμβανον ἔλεγον ἐπίστευον ἐφύλαττον, 3rd singular ἐδυσκόλαινεν ἐθήλαζεν ἐκέλευεν ἐμοίχευεν ἔφασκε ἐφύλαττεν, *applied internally* 1st singular ἐπεβούλευον, contrast 1st singular ἐ-κάθ-ευδον; *with temporal augment* 1st singular ἧκον ἤκουον ἤλπιζον, 3rd singular ἤθελεν ἧκεν ἱκέτευε(ν), *irregular* 2nd singular εἶλκες, 3rd singular εἶχε(ν), *applied internally* 1st singular προσεῖχον

Aorist infinitive ἀποκτεῖναι ἐξαλεῖψαι κελεῦσαι μεῖναι παραγγεῖλαι
Aorist indicative with syllabic augment 1st singular ἐκέλευσα ἔπραξα, 2nd plural ἐτάξατε, *applied internally* 1st singular περιέστρεψα, 3rd singular διέφθειρε;

with temporal augment 3rd singular ἤσχυνε ὕβρισεν, *applied internally* 1st singular ὑπώπτευσα

Aorist subjunctive 2nd singular βασανίσῃς

Aorist optative 3rd singular εἰσαγγείλειε

Aorist participle masculine πατάξας; διαφθείραντα; πείσαντας — feminine ἐπεγείρασα

Future infinitive (middle forms) λήψεσθαι πείσεσθαι

Future indicative 2nd plural εὑρήσετε — 1st singular ἀποκτενῶ, 2nd plural ἐπαρεῖτε; middle forms 1st singular καταλήψομαι, 2nd plural γνώσεσθε, 3rd plural ἐξαμαρτήσονται

Future optative (middle form) 3rd singular καταλήψοιτο

Future participle feminine καθευδήσουσα

A.2 Infinitive in -εσθαι (middle-passive forms)

Present infinitive γίγνεσθαι ἐνεδρεύεσθαι ἐνέχεσθαι ἐπιμέλεσθαι πείθεσθαι; also λοῦσθαι, for λούεσθαι

Present indicative 1st singular βούλομαι ἐξέρχομαι, also οἶμαι = οἴομαι, 2nd singular βούλει, 3rd singular γίγνεται διαφθείρεται εἰσέρχεται ἐφέλκεται οἴεται προσέρχεται, 1st plural εἰσερχόμεθα, 3rd plural παρακελεύονται ψεύδονται

Present subjunctive 3rd singular βούληται

Present participle masculine ἀναμιμνῃσκόμενος βουλόμενος; ψευδόμενοι; βιαζομένους διαπραττομένους; βουλομένοις — feminine ὀργιζομένη; συνεχομένην — neuter γιγνόμενα

Imperfect with syllabic augment 1st singular ἐταραττόμην, 3rd singular ἐγίγνετο ἐδικάζετο; *with temporal augment* 1st singular ὠργιζόμην ᾠχόμην, also ᾤμην for ᾠόμην, 3rd singular ᾤχετο

Aorist middle infinitive ἐνάψασθαι παρασκευάσασθαι παύσασθαι πράξασθαι

Aorist middle indicative with syllabic augment 3rd singular ἐγράψατο; *with temporal augment* 3rd singular ἠμύνατο

Aorist middle subjunctive 2nd singular ψεύσῃ, 3rd singular παύσηται

Aorist middle optative 1st singular διαπραξαίμην

Aorist passive infinitive καταλειφθῆναι συλλεγῆναι

Aorist passive indicative with syllabic augment 1st singular ἐμνήσθην, *applied internally* 1st singular ἀπεκλῄσθην, 3rd singular ἐξεπλάγη; *with temporal augment* 3rd singular ἀπηλλάγη

Aorist passive optative 3rd singular πεισθείη
Aorist passive participle masculine εἰσαρπασθείς πληγείς; βιασθέντων — feminine ὑποπεμφθεῖσα — neuter πραχθέντα

Future middle indicative 2nd singular πεύσει, 3rd singular ἅψεται πεύσεται

B.1.a Infinitive in -ᾶν

Present infinitive ἐᾶν
Present subjunctive 2nd singular πειρᾷς, 3rd singular βοᾷ, 3rd plural ὁρῶσι
Present participle masculine φοιτῶν; ὁρῶντες — feminine τελευτῶσα

Imperfect with syllabic augment 1st singular ἐγέλων ἐσιώπων, 3rd singular ἐβόα ἐφοίτα; *with temporal augment* 1st singular ἠρώτων

Aorist indicative with syllabic augment 3rd singular ἐτελεύτησε ἐτόλμησεν; *with temporal augment* 1st singular ἀπήντησα
Aorist participle masculine ἀπαντήσας

B.1.b Infinitive in -ᾶσθαι (middle-passive forms)

Present participle masculine μηχανώμενοι
Imperfect with temporal augment 1st singular διῃτώμην
Aorist passive participle feminine ὀφθεῖσα
— Here belongs *Present infinitive* χρῆσθαι

B.2.a Infinitive in -εῖν

Present infinitive ἀδικεῖν ἀκολουθεῖν δεῖν δειπνεῖν λυπεῖν ποιεῖν συνδειπνεῖν σωφρονεῖν
Present indicative 1st singular δοκῶ, 3rd singular δεῖ, 3rd plural κατηγοροῦσι ὁμολογοῦσι
Present subjunctive 3rd singular ποιῇ, 1st plural ἀπορῶμεν
Present optative 3rd singular ἀγανακτοίη and δέοι, 3rd plural ψοφοῖεν
Present participle masculine ἐπιτηρῶν συκοφαντῶν ὑπονοῶν; συνδειπνοῦντα; ζητοῦντες; ἐπιδημοῦντας — feminine διοικοῦσα ἐπιτηροῦσα; διακονοῦσαν

Imperfect with syllabic augment 3rd singular ἐψόφει, 1st plural ἐδειπνοῦμεν, *applied internally* 1st singular ἐπεθύμουν συνεχώρουν, 3rd singular συνεδείπνει; *with temporal augment* 1st singular ἠδίκουν ἠσέβουν, 3rd singular κατηγόρει ὡμολόγει — *Double augment* 3rd singular ἠμφεσβήτει ἠντεβόλει

Aorist infinitive γῆμαι
Aorist indicative with syllabic augment 3rd singular ἐποίησε(ν); ἔδοξε, *applied internally* 3rd singular ἐπεχείρησεν
Aorist subjunctive (σκοπεῖν, middle form) 1st plural σκεψώμεθα
Aorist imperative (as above) plural σκέψασθε
Aorist participle masculine δήσας παρακαλέσας; ὤσαντες — feminine ἀκολουθήσασα

Future infinitive ποιήσειν
Future indicative 2nd plural ποιήσετε, 3rd plural ποιήσουσι
Future participle masculine συνδειπνήσοντα

B.2.b Infinitive in -εῖσθαι (middle-passive forms)

Present infinitive ἀδικεῖσθαι μισεῖσθαι
Present indicative 1st singular δέομαι/ ἀφικνοῦμαι ἡγοῦμαι, 3rd singular ἡγεῖται, 3rd plural ἡγοῦνται
Present optative 2nd plural ἡγοῖσθε
Present participle masculine ἐνθυμούμενος ἡγούμενος; ἀδικουμένοις — feminine προσποιουμένη — neuter λυπούμενον

Imperfect with syllabic augment 1st singular ἐποιούμην, 3rd singular ἐτιμωρεῖτο; *with temporal augment* 1st singular ἡγούμην

Aorist middle infinitive διηγήσασθαι
Aorist middle indicative with syllabic augment 2nd singular ἐποιήσω; *with temporal augment* 3rd singular ἡγήσατο, *applied internally* 3rd singular διηγήσατο
Aorist middle subjunctive 3rd singular ποιήσηται
Aorist middle optative 1st singular ποιησαίμην
Aorist middle participle masculine ἡγησάμενοι — feminine ἡγησαμένη
Aorist passive imperative (active in sense) plural ἐνθυμήθητε

B.3.a Infinitive in -οῦν

Present indicative 1st singular ἀξιῶ

Imperfect with temporal augment 1st singular ἠξίουν

Aorist indicative with temporal augment 3rd singular ἠξίωσε

Future indicative 3rd plural ζημιώσουσι

B.3.b Infinitive in -οῦσθαι (passive form)

Aorist passive participle feminine μαστιγωθεῖσαν

C.1 Imperfective (strong) aorists: active

Infinitive διαφυγεῖν εἰπεῖν εἰσαγαγεῖν εἰσελθεῖν ἐμπεσεῖν ἐξευρεῖν μετελθεῖν παθεῖν τυχεῖν
Indicative 1st singular εἶπον ἔλαβον ἦλθον ηὗρον κατέλαβον παρέλαβον, 3rd singular ἐξηῦρεν ἔτυχεν κατέπεσεν, 1st plural εἴδομεν
Subjunctive 2nd singular λάβῃς, 3rd singular ἀποθάνῃ, λάβῃ
Participle masculine ἀγαγών εἰπών ἐλθών ἐξελθών καταφυγών λαβών παραλαβών περιαγαγών; ἐλθόντες λαβόντες; εἰσελθόντας — feminine ἀποθανοῦσα εἰποῦσα λαβοῦσα πεσοῦσα προσελθοῦσα; κατειποῦσαν

C.2 Imperfective (strong) aorists: middle

Infinitive γενέσθαι ἑλέσθαι
Indicative 1st singular ἐπιθόμην ἐπυθόμην ἠγαγόμην ᾐσθόμην, 2nd singular εἵλου, 3rd singular ἐγένετο, 3rd plural διεγένοντο
Subjunctive 1st singular γένωμαι, 3rd singular πύθηται
Participle masculine διαγενομένου ἐρομένου — neuter γενόμενα

D. Verbs in -ναι/ -σθαι ("-μι" verbs)

I εἶναι:
Present infinitive εἶναι
Present indicative 3rd singular ἔστι etc./ ἔξεστι(ν), 3rd plural εἰσί
Present optative 1st singular εἴην, 3rd singular εἴη, 2nd plural εἴητε
Present participle masculine ὤν ὄντος ὄντες ὄντας παρόντων — neuter ἐξόν
Imperfect 1st singular ἦ, 3rd singular ἦν, 3rd plural ἦσαν
Future indicative 3rd singular ἔσται
Future participle neuter ἐσομένων
— Cf. (χρῆναι ~ χρὴ εἶναι):
Present indicative 3rd singular χρή

I Others, active forms:

Present infinitive ἀπιέναι εἰσιέναι

Present indicative 3rd singular προστίθησι

Present subjunctive 3rd singular διδῷ

Present optative 3rd singular προσίοι

Present participle masculine ἀπιών εἰσιών, προϊόντος, ἰόντι, εἰσιόντες; also τιθείς — feminine ἀπιοῦσα

Imperfect 1st singular εἰσῇα, 3rd singular ἀπῄει εἰσῄει; 1st singular ἔφην, 3rd singular ἔφη

Aorist infinitive δοῦναι/ θεῖναι; ἀπολέσαι/ ἐπιδεῖξαι

Aorist indicative 1st singular παρέδωκα, 3rd singular ἐπέθηκε; 3rd singular ἀνέῳξεν/ ἀπώλεσεν

Aorist participle masculine ἀφείς — feminine ἀναστᾶσα

— Also aorists βῆναι (βαίνειν) and γνῶναι (γιγνώσκειν): *Indicative* 3rd singular κατέγνω, *Imperative* singular ἀνάγνωθι, plural ἀνάβητε, *Participle* masculine καταβάς ἀναβάντες

Future indicative 1st singular ἐπιδείξω; also, from εἰδέναι, 3rd plural (middle form) εἴσονται

III Others, middle-passive forms:

δύνασθαι: *Present participle* masculine δυναμένους *Imperfect* 3rd singular ἐδύνατο *Aorist subjunctive* 1st singular δυνηθῶ — Also *Present infinitive* τίθεσθαι *Aorist infinitive* ἀποσβεσθῆναι *Present optative* 3rd singular προσίοιτο

APPENDIX B

CHECKLIST OF VERBS

This alphabetical list provides a key to all verbal forms in the speech with the exception of perfect/ pluperfect, examined elsewhere.

ἀγαγών (ἄγειν) *Active* Aorist participle masculine nominative singular

ἀγανακτοίη (ἀγανακτεῖν) *Active* Present optative 3rd singular

ἀδικεῖν [3x] *Active* Present infinitive — ἀδικεῖσθαι *Passive* Present infinitive — ἀδικουμένοις [2x] *Passive* Present participle masculine dative plural

αἰσχύνῃ (αἰσχύνειν) *Active* Present subjunctive 3rd singular

ἀκολουθεῖν *Active* Present infinitive — ἀκολουθήσασα *Active* Aorist participle feminine nominative singular

ἀκούετε [2x] (ἀκούειν) *Active* Present indicative 2nd plural — ἀκούουσι *Active* Present participle masculine dative plural

ἁμαρτάνειν *Active* Present infinitive

ἀναβάντες (ἀναβαίνειν) *Active* Aorist participle masculine nominative plural — ἀνάβητε [2x] *Active* Aorist imperative plural

ἀνάγνωθι [3x] (ἀναγιγνώσκειν) *Active* Aorist imperative singular

ἀναμιμνησκόμενος (ἀναμιμνῄσκεσθαι) *Middle* Present participle masculine nominative singular

ἀναστᾶσα (ἀνιστάναι) *Active* Aorist participle feminine nominative singular

ἀνέῳξεν (ἀνοιγνύναι) *Active* Aorist indicative 3rd singular

ἀξιῶ [2x] (ἀξιοῦν) *Active* Present indicative 1st singular

ἀπαντήσας (ἀπαντᾶν) *Active* Aorist participle masculine nominative singular

ἀπεκλῄσθην (ἀποκλείειν) *Passive* Aorist indicative 1st singular

ἀπῄει (ἀπιέναι) *Active* Imperfect 3rd singular

ἀπηλλάγη (ἀπαλλάττειν) *Passive* Aorist indicative 3rd singular

ἀπήντησα (ἀπαντᾶν) *Active* Aorist indicative 1st singular

ἀπιέναι [2x] *Active* Present infinitive — ἀπιοῦσα *Active* Present participle feminine nominative singular — ἀπιών [2x] *Active* Present participle masculine nominative singular

ἀποθάνῃ (ἀποθνῄσκειν) *Active* Aorist subjunctive 3rd singular — ἀποθανοῦσα *Active* Aorist participle feminine nominative singular

ἀποκτεῖναι (ἀποκτείνειν) *Active* Aorist infinitive — ἀποκτείνειν *Active* Present infinitive — ἀποκτενῶ *Active* Future indicative 1st singular

ἀπολέσαι [2x] (ἀπολλύναι) *Active* Aorist infinitive

ἀπορῶμεν (ἀπορεῖν) *Active* Present subjunctive 1st plural

ἀποσβεσθῆναι (ἀποσβεννύναι) *Passive* Aorist infinitive

ἀποτίνειν *Active* Present infinitive

ἀπώλεσεν (ἀπολλύναι) *Active* Aorist indicative 3rd singular

ἀφείς (ἀφιέναι/ -ίημι) *Active* Aorist participle masculine nominative singular

ἀφικνοῦμαι (ἀφικνεῖσθαι) *Middle* Present indicative 1st singular

ἅψεται (ἅπτεσθαι) *Middle* Future indicative 3rd singular

βαδίζουσαν [2x] (βαδίζειν) *Active* Present participle feminine accusative singular

βασανίσῃς (βασανίζειν) *Active* Aorist subjunctive 2nd singular βιαζομένους (βιάζεσθαι) *Middle* Present participle masculine accusative plural — βιασθέντων (βιάζειν) *Passive* Aorist participle masculine genitive plural

βοᾷ (βοᾶν) *Active* Present subjunctive 3rd singular

βούλει (βούλεσθαι) *Middle* Present indicative 2nd singular — βούληται *Middle* Present subjunctive 3rd singular — βούλομαι [2x] *Middle* Present indicative 1st singular — βουλομένοις *Middle* Present participle masculine dative plural — βουλόμενος *Middle* Present participle masculine nominative singular

γενέσθαι [4x] (γίγνεσθαι) *Middle* Aorist infinitive — γενόμενα *Middle* Aorist participle neuter accusative plural — γένωμαι *Middle* Aorist subjunctive 1st singular

γῆμαι (γαμεῖν) *Active* Aorist infinitive

γίγνεσθαι *Middle* Present infinitive — γίγνεται *Middle* Present indicative 3rd singular — γιγνόμενα *Middle* Present participle neuter accusative plural

γνώσεσθε (γιγνώσκειν) *Middle form* Future indicative 2nd plural

δεῖ [3x] (δεῖν) *Active* Present indicative 3rd singular — δεῖν [2x] *Active* Present infinitive

δειπνεῖν *Active* Present infinitive

δέοι (δεῖν) *Active* Present optative 3rd singular

δέομαι (δεῖσθαι) *Middle* Present indicative 1st singular

δήσας (δεῖν) *Active* Aorist participle masculine nominative singular

διαγενομένου (διαγίγνεσθαι) *Middle* Aorist participle masculine genitive singular

διακονοῦσαν (διακονεῖν) *Active* Present participle feminine accusative singular

διαπραξαίμην (διαπράττεσθαι) *Middle* Aorist optative 1st singular — διαπραττομένους *Middle* Present participle masculine accusative plural διαφθείραντα (διαφθείρειν) *Active* Aorist participle masculine accusative singular — διαφθείρειν *Active* Present infinitive — διαφθείρεται *Passive* Present indicative 3rd singular

διαφυγεῖν (διαφεύγειν) *Active* Aorist infinitive

διδῷ (διδόναι) *Active* Present subjunctive 3rd singular

διεγένοντο (διαγίγνεσθαι) *Middle* Aorist indicative 3rd plural

διέφθειρε (διαφθείρειν) *Active* Aorist indicative 3rd singular

διηγήσασθαι [2x] (διηγεῖσθαι) *Middle* Aorist infinitive — διηγήσατο *Middle* Aorist indicative 3rd singular

διῃτώμην (διαιτᾶσθαι) *Middle* Imperfect 1st singular

δικάζειν *Active* Present infinitive

διοικοῦσα (διοικεῖν) *Active* Present participle feminine nominative singular

δοκῶ [3x] (δοκεῖν) *Active* Present indicative 1st singular

δοῦναι (διδόναι) *Active* Aorist infinitive

δυναμένους (δύνασθαι) *Middle* Present participle masculine accusative plural — δυνηθῶ *Middle in passive form* Aorist subjunctive 1st singular

ἐᾶν *Active* Present infinitive

ἐβάδιζον [2x] (βαδίζειν) *Active* Imperfect 1st singular

ἐβόα (βοᾶν) *Active* Imperfect 3rd singular

ἐγέλων (γελᾶν) *Active* Imperfect 1st singular

ἐγένετο [2x] (γίγνεσθαι) *Middle* Aorist indicative 3rd singular — ἐγίγνετο *Middle* Imperfect 3rd singular

ἐγράψατο (γράφεσθαι) *Middle* Aorist indicative 3rd singular ἐδειπνοῦμεν (δειπνεῖν) *Active* Imperfect 1st plural

ἐδικάζετο (δικάζεσθαι) *Middle* Imperfect 3rd singular

ἔδοξε [3x] (δοκεῖν) *Active* Aorist indicative 3rd singular

ἐδύνατο (δύνασθαι) *Middle* Imperfect 3rd singular

ἐδυσκόλαινεν (δυσκολαίνειν) *Active* Imperfect 3rd singular

ἐθέλῃ (ἐθέλειν) *Active* Present subjunctive 3rd singular

ἐθήλαζεν (θηλάζειν) *Active* Imperfect 3rd singular

εἴδομεν (ὁρᾶν) *Active* Aorist indicative 1st plural

εἴη [4x] (εἶναι) *Active* Present optative 3rd singular — εἴην *Active* Present optative 1st singular — εἴητε *Active* Present optative 2nd plural

εἷλκες (ἕλκειν) *Active* Imperfect 2nd singular

εἵλου (αἱρεῖσθαι) *Middle* Aorist indicative 2nd singular

εἶναι [11x] *Active* Present infinitive

εἰπεῖν (λέγειν) *Active* Aorist infinitive — εἶπον [4x] *Active* Aorist indicative 1st singular — εἰποῦσα *Active* Aorist participle feminine nominative singular — εἰπών [2x] *Active* Aorist participle masculine nominative singular

εἰσαγαγεῖν (εἰσάγειν) *Active* Aorist infinitive

εἰσαγγείλειε (εἰσαγγέλλειν) *Active* Aorist optative 3rd singular

εἰσαρπασθείς (εἰσαρπάζειν) *Passive* Aorist participle masculine nominative singular

εἰσελθεῖν (εἰσιέναι/ -έρχομαι) *Active* Aorist infinitive — εἰσελθόντας *Active* Aorist participle masculine accusative plural — εἰσέρχεται *Middle* Present indicative 3rd singular — εἰσερχόμεθα *Middle* Present indicative 1st plural εἰσῇα (εἰσιέναι) *Active* Imperfect 1st singular — εἰσῄει [2x] *Active* Imperfect 3rd singular

εἰσί (εἶναι) *Active* Present indicative 3rd plural

εἰσιέναι *Active* Present infinitive — εἰσιόντες *Active* Present participle masculine nominative plural — εἰσιών [2x] *Active* Present participle masculine nominative singular

εἴσονται (εἰδέναι) *Middle form* Future indicative 3rd plural

εἶχε(ν) [4x] (ἔχειν) *Active* Imperfect 3rd singular

ἐκάθευδον [2x] (καθεύδειν) *Active* Imperfect 1st singular

ἐκβάλλειν *Active* Present infinitive

ἐκέλευεν (κελεύειν) *Active* Imperfect 3rd singular — ἐκέλευον [5x] *Active* Imperfect 1st singular — ἐκέλευσα *Active* Aorist indicative 1st singular

ἐκινδύνευον (κινδυνεύειν) *Active* Imperfect 1st singular

ἔλαβον (λαμβάνειν) *Active* Aorist 1st singular — ἐλάμβανον *Active* Imperfect 1st singular

ἔλεγον (λέγειν) *Active* Imperfect 1st singular

ἑλέσθαι (αἱρεῖσθαι) *Middle* Aorist infinitive

ἐλθόντες [2x] (ἰέναι/ ἔρχομαι) *Active* Aorist participle masculine nominative plural — ἐλθών *Active* Aorist participle masculine nominative singular

ἐμνήσθην (μιμνῄσκεσθαι) *Middle* Aorist indicative 1st singular

ἐμοίχευεν [2x] (μοιχεύειν) *Active* Imperfect 3rd singular

ἐμπεσεῖν (ἐμπίπτειν) *Active* Aorist infinitive

ἐνάψασθαι (ἐνάπτεσθαι) *Middle* Aorist infinitive

ἐνεδρεύεσθαι (ἐνεδρεύειν) *Passive* Present infinitive

ἐνέχεσθαι (ἐνέχειν) *Passive* Present infinitive

ἐνθυμήθητε (ἐνθυμεῖσθαι) *Middle* Aorist imperative plural — ἐνθυμούμενος [2x] *Middle* Present participle masculine nominative singular

ἐξαλεῖψαι (ἐξαλείφειν) *Active* Aorist infinitive

ἐξαμαρτάνειν *Active* Present infinitive — ἐξαμαρτήσονται *Middle form* Future indicative 3rd plural

ἐξελθών (ἐξιέναι/ -έρχομαι) *Active* Aorist participle masculine nominative singular

ἐξεπλάγη (ἐκπλήττειν) *Passive* Aorist indicative 3rd singular

ἐξέρχομαι (ἐξιέναι/ -έρχομαι) *Middle* Present indicative 1st singular

ἔξεστι(ν) [2x] (ἐξεῖναι) *Active* Present indicative 3rd singular

ἐξευρεῖν (ἐξευρίσκειν) *Active* Aorist infinitive — ἐξηῦρεν *Active* Aorist indicative 3rd singular

ἐξόν (ἐξεῖναι) *Active* Present participle neuter accusative singular

ἐπαρεῖτε (ἐπαίρειν) *Active* Future indicative 2nd plural

ἐπεβούλευον (ἐπιβουλεύειν) *Active* Imperfect 1st singular

ἐπεγείρασα (ἐπεγείρειν) *Active* Aorist participle feminine nominative singular

ἐπέθηκε (ἐπιτιθέναι) *Active* Aorist indicative 3rd singular

ἐπεθύμουν [2x] (ἐπιθυμεῖν) *Active* Imperfect 1st singular

ἐπεχείρησεν (ἐπιχειρεῖν) *Active* Aorist indicative 3rd singular

ἐπιβουλεύουσι (ἐπιβουλεύειν) *Active* Present indicative 3rd plural

ἐπιδεῖξαι [2x] (ἐπιδεικνύναι) *Active* Aorist infinitive — ἐπιδείξω [2x] *Active* Future indicative 1st singular ἐπιδημοῦντας [2x] (ἐπιδημεῖν) *Active* Present participle masculine accusative plural

ἐπιθόμην (πείθεσθαι) *Middle* Aorist indicative 1st singular

ἐπιμέλεσθαι *Middle* Present infinitive

ἐπίστευον (πιστεύειν) *Active* Imperfect 1st singular

ἐπιτηδευόντων (ἐπιτηδεύειν) *Active* Present participle masculine genitive plural — ἐπιτηδεύουσιν *Active* Present participle masculine dative plural

ἐπιτηροῦσα (ἐπιτηρεῖν) *Active* Present participle feminine nominative singular — ἐπιτηρῶν *Active* Present participle masculine nominative singular

ἐποίησε(ν) [3x] (ποιεῖν) *Active* Aorist indicative 3rd singular — ἐποιήσω (ποιεῖσθαι) *Middle* Aorist indicative 2nd singular — ἐποιούμην *Middle* Imperfect 1st singular

ἔπραξα (πράττειν) *Active* Aorist indicative 1st singular

ἐπυθόμην (πυνθάνεσθαι) *Middle* Aorist indicative 1st singular

ἐρομένου (ἐρέσθαι) [aorist infinitive] *Middle* Aorist participle masculine genitive singular

ἐσιώπων (σιωπᾶν) *Active* Imperfect 1st singular

ἐσομένων (εἶναι) *Middle form* Future participle neuter genitive plural — ἔσται *Middle form* Future indicative 3rd singular — ἔστι/ ἐστί/ ἐστι [7x] *Active* Present indicative 3rd singular

ἐτάξατε (τάττειν) *Active* Aorist indicative 2nd plural

ἐταραττόμην (ταράττειν) *Passive* Imperfect 1st singular

ἐτελεύτησε (τελευτᾶν) *Active* Aorist indicative 3rd singular

ἐτιμωρεῖτο (τιμωρεῖσθαι) *Middle* Imperfect 3rd singular

ἐτόλμησεν (τολμᾶν) *Active* Aorist indicative 3rd singular

ἔτυχεν (τυγχάνειν) *Active* Aorist indicative 3rd singular

εὑρήσετε (εὑρίσκειν) *Active* Future indicative 2nd plural

ἔφασκε (φάσκειν) *Active* Imperfect 3rd singular

ἐφέλκεται (ἐφέλκεσθαι) *Middle* Present indicative 3rd singular

ἔφη [3x] (φάναι) *Active* Imperfect 3rd singular — ἔφην *Active* Imperfect 1st singular

ἐφοίτα (φοιτᾶν) *Active* Imperfect 3rd singular

ἐφύλαττεν (φυλάττειν) *Active* Imperfect 3rd singular — ἐφύλαττον *Active* Imperfect 1st singular

ἔχει [2x] (ἔχειν) *Active* Present indicative 3rd singular — ἔχειν [3x] *Active* Present infinitive — ἔχοιτε *Active* Present optative 2nd plural — ἔχον *Active* Present participle neuter nominative singular — ἔχοντας *Active* Present participle masculine accusative plural — ἔχων *Active* Present participle masculine nominative singular

ἐψόφει (ψοφεῖν) *Active* Imperfect 3rd singular

ζημιώσουσι (ζημιοῦν) *Active* Future indicative 3rd plural

ζητοῦντες (ζητεῖν) *Active* Present participle masculine nominative plural

ἦ [6x] (εἶναι) *Active* Imperfect 1st singular

ἠγαγόμην (ἄγεσθαι) *Middle* Aorist indicative 1st singular

ἡγεῖται (ἡγεῖσθαι) *Middle* Present indicative 3rd singular — ἡγησαμένη *Middle* Aorist participle feminine nominative singular — ἡγησάμενοι *Middle* Aorist participle masculine nominative plural — ἡγήσατο [2x] *Middle* Aorist indicative 3rd singular — ἡγοῖσθε *Middle* Present optative 2nd plural — ἡγοῦμαι [2x] *Middle* Present indicative 1st singular — ἡγούμενος [2x] *Middle* Present participle masculine nominative singular — ἡγούμην [3x] *Middle* Imperfect 1st singular — ἡγοῦνται *Middle* Present indicative 3rd plural

ἠδίκουν (ἀδικεῖν) *Active* Imperfect 1st singular

ἤθελεν (ἐθέλειν) *Active* Imperfect 3rd singular

ἧκεν (ἥκειν) *Active* Imperfect 3rd singular — ἧκον *Active* Imperfect 1st singular — ἥκοντα *Active* Present participle masculine accusative singular

ἤκουον (ἀκούειν) *Active* Imperfect 1st singular

ἥκων (ἥκειν) *Active* Present participle masculine nominative singular

ἦλθον (ἰέναι/ ἔρχομαι) *Active* Aorist indicative 1st singular

ἤλπιζον (ἐλπίζειν) *Active* Imperfect 1st singular

ἠμύνατο (ἀμύνεσθαι) *Middle* Aorist 3rd singular

ἠμφεσβήτει (ἀμφισβητεῖν) *Active* Imperfect 3rd singular

ἦν [12x] (εἶναι) *Active* Imperfect 3rd singular

ἠντεβόλει [2x] (ἀντιβολεῖν) *Active* Imperfect 3rd singular

ἠξίουν (ἀξιοῦν) *Active* Imperfect 1st singular — ἠξίωσε *Active* Aorist indicative 3rd singular

ἠρώτων (ἐρωτᾶν) *Active* Imperfect 1st singular

ἦσαν (εἶναι) *Active* Imperfect 3rd plural

ἠσέβουν (ἀσεβεῖν) *Active* Imperfect 1st singular

ᾐσθόμην (αἰσθάνεσθαι) *Middle* Aorist indicative 1st singular

ᾔσχυνε (αἰσχύνειν) *Active* Aorist indicative 3rd singular

ηὗρον (εὑρίσκειν) *Active* Aorist indicative 1st singular

θεῖναι (τιθέναι) *Active* Aorist infinitive

ἱκέτευε(ν) [2x] (ἱκετεύειν) *Active* Imperfect 3rd singular

ἰόντι (ἰέναι) *Active* Present participle masculine dative singular καθευδήσουσα (καθεύδειν) *Active* Future participle feminine nominative singular

καταβαίνουσα (καταβαίνειν) *Active* Present participle feminine nominative singular

καταβάλλω (καταβάλλειν) *Active* Present indicative 1st singular

καταβάς (καταβαίνειν) *Active* Aorist participle masculine nominative singular

καταγιγνώσκειν *Active* Present infinitive

καταισχύνουσι (καταισχύνειν) *Active* Present participle masculine dative plural

καταλειφθῆναι (καταλείπειν) *Passive* Aorist infinitive

καταλήψοιτο (καταλαμβάνειν) *Middle form* Future optative 3rd singular — καταλήψομαι *id.* Future indicative 1st singular

καταφυγών (καταφεύγειν) *Active* Aorist participle masculine nominative singular

κατέγνω (καταγιγνώσκειν) *Active* Aorist indicative 3rd singular

κατειποῦσαν (καταλέγειν) *Active* Aorist participle feminine accusative singular

κατέλαβον [2x] (καταλαμβάνειν) *Active* Aorist indicative 1st singular

κατέπεσεν (καταπίπτειν) *Active* Aorist indicative 3rd singular

κατηγόρει (κατηγορεῖν) *Active* Imperfect 3rd singular — κατηγοροῦσι *Active* Present indicative 3rd plural

κελεύει (κελεύειν) *Active* Present indicative 3rd singular — κελεύειν *Active* Present infinitive — κελεύουσι [3x] *Active* Present indicative 3rd plural — κελεῦσαι *Active* Aorist infinitive

κινδυνεύῃ (κινδυνεύειν) *Active* Present subjunctive 3rd singular — κινδυνεύω *Active* Present indicative 1st singular

κλᾶον (κλάειν) *Active* Present participle neuter nominative singular λάβῃ (λαμβάνειν) *Active* Aorist subjunctive 3rd singular — λάβῃς *Active* Aorist subjunctive 2nd singular — λαβόντες *Active* Aorist participle masculine nominative plural — λαβοῦσα *Active* Aorist participle feminine nominative singular — λαβών [2x] *Active* Aorist participle masculine nominative singular — λαμβάνειν [2x] *Active* Present infinitive — λαμβάνων *Active* Present participle masculine nominative singular

λέγε (λέγειν) *Active* Present imperative singular — λέγειν *Active* Present infinitive — λέγουσι *Active* Present indicative 3rd plural — λέγων *Active* Present participle masculine nominative singular — λέγωσι *Active* Present subjunctive 3rd plural

λήψεσθαι (λαμβάνειν) *Middle form* Future infinitive

λοῦσθαι = λούεσθαι *Passive* Present infinitive

λυπεῖν *Active* Present infinitive — λυπούμενον *Passive* Present participle neuter nominative singular

μαστιγωθεῖσαν (μαστιγοῦν) *Passive* Aorist participle feminine accusative singular

μεθύων (μεθύειν) *Active* Present participle masculine nominative singular

μεῖναι (μένειν) *Active* Aorist infinitive

μετελθεῖν [2x] (μετιέναι/ -έρχομαι) *Active* Aorist infinitive

μηχανώμενοι (μηχανᾶσθαι) *Middle* Present participle masculine nominative plural

μισεῖσθαι (μισεῖν) *Passive* Present infinitive

νόμιζε (νομίζειν) *Active* Present imperative singular — νομίζουσα *Active* Present participle feminine nominative singular — νομίζω [2x] *Active* Present indicative 1st singular

οἴεται (οἴεσθαι) *Middle* Present indicative 3rd singular — οἶμαι [2x] (= οἴομαι) *Middle* Present indicative 1st singular

ὁμολογοῦσι (ὁμολογεῖν) *Active* Present indicative 3rd plural ὄντας (εἶναι) *Active* Present participle masculine accusative plural — ὄντες *Active* Present participle masculine nominative plural — ὄντος *Active* Present participle masculine genitive singular

ὀργιζομένη (ὀργίζεσθαι) *Middle* Present participle feminine nominative singular

ὁρῶντες (ὁρᾶν) *Active* Present participle masculine nominative plural — ὁρῶσι *Active* Present subjunctive 3rd plural

ὀφείλειν *Active* Present infinitive

ὀφθεῖσα (ὁρᾶν) *Passive* Aorist participle feminine nominative singular

παθεῖν (πάσχειν) *Active* Aorist infinitive

παίζειν *Active* Present infinitive

παραβαίνων (παραβαίνειν) *Active* Present participle masculine nominative singular

παραγγεῖλαι [2x] (παραγγέλλειν) *Active* Aorist infinitive

παρακαλέσας (παρακαλεῖν) *Active* Aorist participle masculine nominative singular

παρακελεύονται (παρακελεύεσθαι) *Middle* Present indicative 3rd plural

παραλαβών (παραλαμβάνειν) *Active* Aorist participle masculine nominative singular

παραλείπων (παραλείπειν) *Active* Present participle masculine nominative singular

παρασκευάζουσι (παρασκευάζειν) *Active* Present indicative 3rd plural — παρασκευάσασθαι (παρασκευάζεσθαι) *Middle* Aorist infinitive

παρέδωκα (παραδιδόναι) *Active* Aorist indicative 1st singular

παρέλαβον (παραλαμβάνειν) *Active* Aorist indicative 1st singular

παρόντων (παρεῖναι) *Active* Present participle masculine genitive plural πατάξας (πατάσσειν) *Active* Aorist participle masculine nominative singular

παύσασθαι (παύεσθαι) *Middle* Aorist infinitive — παύσηται *Middle* Aorist subjunctive 3rd singular

πείθεσθαι *Middle* Present infinitive — πείθοντας (πείθειν) *Active* Present participle masculine accusative plural

πειρᾷς (πειρᾶν) *Active* Present subjunctive 2nd singular

πείσαντας (πείθειν) *Active* Aorist participle masculine accusative plural

πείσεσθαι (πάσχειν) *Middle form* Future infinitive

πεισθείη (πείθειν) *Passive* Aorist optative 3rd singular

περιαγαγών (περιάγειν) *Active* Aorist participle masculine nominative singular

περιέστρεψα (περιστρέφειν) *Active* Aorist indicative 1st singular

περιτρέχειν *Active* Present infinitive

πεσοῦσα (πίπτειν) *Active* Aorist participle feminine nominative singular

πεύσει (πυνθάνεσθαι) *Middle* Future indicative 2nd singular — πεύσεται *Middle* Future indicative 3rd singular

πληγείς (πλήττειν) *Passive* Aorist participle masculine nominative singular

ποιεῖν [4x] *Active* Present infinitive — ποιῇ *Active* Present subjunctive 3rd singular — ποιησαίμην (ποιεῖσθαι) *Middle* Aorist optative 1st singular — ποιήσειν (ποιεῖν) *Active* Future infinitive — ποιήσετε *Active* Future indicative 2nd plural — ποιήσηται (ποιεῖσθαι) *Middle* Aorist subjunctive 3rd singular — ποιήσουσι (ποιεῖν) *Active* Future indicative 3rd plural

πράξασθαι (πράττεσθαι) *Middle* Aorist infinitive — πράττοντας (πράττειν) *Active* Present participle masculine accusative plural — πράττοντες [2x] *Active* Present participle masculine nominative plural — πραττόντων *Active* Present participle masculine genitive plural — πράττων *Active* Present participle masculine nominative singular — πραχθέντα *Passive* Aorist participle neuter accusative plural προϊόντος (προιέναι) *Active* Present participle masculine genitive singular

προσεῖχον (προσέχειν) *Active* Imperfect 1st singular

προσελθοῦσα (προσιέναι/ -έρχομαι) *Active* Aorist participle feminine nominative singular — προσέρχεται *Middle* Present indicative 3rd singular

προσίοι (προσιέναι/ -έρχομαι) *Active* Present optative 3rd singular

προσίοιτο (προσίεσθαι) *Middle* Present optative 3rd singular

προσποιουμένη (προσποιεῖσθαι) *Middle* Present participle feminine nominative singular

προστίθησι (προστιθέναι) *Active* Present indicative 3rd singular

προσφέρων (προσφέρειν) *Active* Present participle masculine nominative singular

πύθηται (πυνθάνεσθαι) *Middle* Aorist subjunctive 3rd singular

σκέψασθε [3x] (σκοπεῖν) *Middle form* Aorist imperative plural — σκεψώμεθα *id.* Aorist subjunctive 1st plural

συκοφαντῶν (συκοφαντεῖν) *Active* Present participle masculine nominative singular

συλλεγῆναι (συλλέγειν) *Passive* Aorist infinitive

συνδειπνεῖν *Active* Present infinitive — συνδειπνήσοντα *Active* Future participle masculine accusative singular — συνδειπνοῦντα *Active* Present participle masculine accusative singular — συνεδείπνει *Active* Imperfect 3rd singular

συνεχομένην (συνέχειν) *Passive* Present participle feminine accusative singular

συνεχώρουν (συγχωρεῖν) *Active* Imperfect 1st singular

σωφρονεῖν *Active* Present infinitive

τελευτῶσα (τελευτᾶν) *Active* Present participle feminine nominative singular τιθείς (τιθέναι) *Active* Present participle masculine nominative singular — τίθεσθαι *Middle* Present infinitive

τυγχάνει (τυγχάνειν) *Active* Present indicative 3rd singular — τυγχάνειν [2x] *Active* Present infinitive — τυγχάνουσιν *Active* Present indicative 3rd plural — τυχεῖν *Active* Aorist infinitive

ὑβρίζει (ὑβρίζειν) *Active* Present indicative 3rd singular — ὑβρίζων *Active* Present participle masculine nominative singular — ὕβρισεν *Active* Aorist indicative 3rd singular

ὑπονοῶν (ὑπονοεῖν) *Active* Present participle masculine nominative singular

ὑποπεμφθεῖσα (ὑποπέμπειν) *Passive* Aorist participle feminine nominative singular

ὑπώπτευσα (ὑποπτεύειν) *Active* Aorist indicative 1st singular

φάσκειν *Active* Present infinitive — φάσκωσιν *Active* Present subjunctive 3rd plural

φοιτῶν (φοιτᾶν) *Active* Present participle masculine nominative singular

φράζει (φράζειν) *Active* Present indicative 3rd singular

φυλάττοντας (φυλάττειν) *Active* Present participle masculine accusative plural

χαίρειν *Active* Present infinitive

χρή (χρῆναι) *Active* Present indicative 3rd singular

χρῆσθαι *Middle* Present infinitive

ψευδόμενοι (ψεύδεσθαι) *Middle* Present participle masculine nominative plural — ψεύδονται *Middle* Present indicative 3rd plural — ψεύσῃ *Middle* Aorist subjunctive 2nd singular

ψοφοῖεν (ψοφεῖν) *Active* Present optative 3rd plural

ᾤμην (= ῴόμην) (οἴεσθαι) *Middle* Imperfect 1st singular

ὡμολόγει [3x] (ὁμολογεῖν) *Active* Imperfect 3rd singular

ὤν [3x] (εἶναι) *Active* Present participle masculine nominative singular

ὠργιζόμην (ὀργίζεσθαι) *Middle* Imperfect 1st singular

ὤσαντες (ὠθεῖν) *Active* Aorist participle masculine nominative plural

ᾤχετο [3x] (οἴχεσθαι) *Middle* Imperfect 3rd singular — ᾠχόμην *Middle* Imperfect 1st singular

CPSIA information can be obtained
at www.ICGtesting.com
Printed in the USA
LVHW021711130121
676408LV00013B/316

9 781853 995378